Journey

Into the

Apostolic

Journey
Into the
Apostolic

Bill Easter

Transcription by Carol and Dan Vaisanen

Editing and layout by Carol Vaisanen

Copy editing by Dan Vaisanen

Photography by Natalie Kleese, Amara Studio

ISBN-978-0-9855447-3-7

PUBLISHED BY GLOBAL APOSTOLIC REVIVAL NETWORK
www.garn.tv

Printed in the United States of America

Spiritual Dedication

To my Heavenly Father.

To my King, Jesus.

To my Friend, Holy Spirit.

I can do nothing without each of you.

Earthly Dedication

To my awesome, beautiful wife Denise.

To my wonderful daughter Rhiannon.

To my awesome daughter and son-in-law, Tara and Jonathan Landis.

To my Grandsons Josiah and Elisha for whom I am building a heritage.

To Mom and Dad, the best parents ever.

I love you guys. Thanks for hanging in there during this *Journey* and encouraging me along the way.

Acknowledgement

I want to thank men and women of God like John Kilpatrick, Randy Clark, Bill Johnson, David Hogan, Patricia King, and Heidi Baker, who have carried the Fires of Revival and been a big influence in my life through their books and ministry.

In Loving Memory

Jeff and Dawn Norris, pastors of New Life Fellowship, Winfield, Alabama, left this world too early. I am ever grateful for their love and dedication to the Lord, and for encouraging me to continue on the path God had set before me. They are greatly missed.

Table of Contents

Editors' Foreword

Bill Easter is a man on a journey. In 1989, Bill surrendered his life to Jesus Christ and became a new man with God setting his feet on a path with one divine appointment after another. Bill has been hungry to know more of God, having determined to follow the Lord wherever the journey might take him.

One providential day in July 2010, Bill's journey led him to a small church in Golden, Colorado, where, by Divine appointment, his life intersected with ours in such a way that has changed us forever. It was almost instantaneous that, upon hearing some of Bill's adventures, we offered to help him write his story. Along with the compilation and editing of the manuscript came the forging of an eternal friendship as together with Bill we have sought first the Kingdom of God.

During the journey of writing *Journey Into The Apostolic*, God invaded our lives in ways beyond what can be described in this foreword. Suffice it to say we quickly became aware that God was in the writing of this story.

Journey Into The Apostolic is a relevant book written for "such a time as this" and is certain to play an important role in ushering in the Kingdom of God to a lost and dying world in helping set the stage for the Bride of Christ to meet her Bridegroom.

It is our prayer that the Lord will bless your life as you read through this book and that, along with us, you will give praise to God for bringing Bill Easter and his *Journey* into your life. To God be the glory.

Carol and Dan Vaisanen
Aurora, Colorado
June 2012

1

Just A Sinner

Man, God really messed up my life. The year was 1997. I was hungry for God and the fire of revival was burning in my heart. I read every book I could find on revival. I wanted to know what brought revival, what the different characteristics of revival were, and what characterized the mighty men and women of God who ushered it in.

I had visited the Brownsville Revival in Pensacola, Florida, where I was powerfully touched by God. There the Lord turned my life upside down. I saw things happen I had never seen before. It was a raw demonstration of God's power. I had been in revivals before, but in this revival things were happening at a different level. I would see people become brand new Christians, receive extra prayer, and then head down to the restaurant Shoney's carrying the glory of God, lay hands on the sick, and watch them recover. These new Christians had no former training and yet were doing the stuff that early Christians did.

At the time, I was pastoring First Assembly of God in Bolivar, Tennessee. Having received special prayer at Brownsville, the revival anointing that was there had come upon me. When I returned to my church, I found a great increase in the presence of God. The same powerful things that were happening at Brownsville began to happen at my church. As I laid hands on people to pray for them, they would fall under the mighty hand of God. Some broke out in laughter that lasted for hours. Others wept and travailed in prayer. Some shook violently, their natural bodies unable to withstand the power of God that had come upon them. I was witnessing things I had previously only read about in books having to do with moves of God.

Our church in Bolivar experienced a move of God that lasted for twenty-five weeks in nightly meetings averaging around a hundred and twenty-five people, during which time a hundred people were saved, a hundred and fifty were baptized in water, and over a hundred were filled with the Holy Spirit.

When God is moving like this you don't get much sleep as a minister under the anointing. You lie down but can feel God's power surging through your body like electricity and are unable to sleep. At times you want to tell God to back off on the power, but then you think, *This is what I've been praying for ... to carry God's power in such a way that it would affect the lives of others.* When heaven invades earth, you've got things to do. People want to be ministered to. You're there for them early in the morning until late at night. I became weary in well-doing and would long to find a quiet spot just to spend time in the presence of the Father. He became so real to me. His Word had come alive like never before.

I had been searching for the Acts 1:8 power dynamics or, *dunamis*—the power to perform miracles, moral power, and the power residing in armies. We are dangerous to the devil when we walk in this kind of power. The sick are healed, demons are cast out, the dead are raised, and the gospel is preached with power. In Matthew 11:12 we read that "the kingdom of heaven suffers violence, and violent men take it by force." Holy Ghost power compels believers to make a forceful takeover of the devil's kingdom. I was blessed now to not only have read about the hand of God moving mightily on the earth, but to be an eye witness to it.

It's hard to explain what it's like when heaven invades earth. Demons manifest and must be cast out. Spiritual warfare increases with intensity. Suddenly, you find that you've been moved to the front lines of a major battle — a battle for the souls of men. Yet, no matter how great the battle or how tired you get, it is worth it all just to find yourself in the presence of the Lord. Like King David said, a day in His courts is better than a thousand elsewhere (see Psalm 84:10).

Despite the regular revival meetings in Bolivar eventually coming to an end, I was still hungry for God. I had experienced something I could not live without: His manifest presence. If any revival meetings were going on in my part of the country, I was there. For the next eight years I would be haunted by the question of what was different about the revival at Brownsville that had touched my church in Bolivar so powerfully compared to revivals in the past. I just couldn't put my finger on it.

One night, I visited a church in Somerville, Tennessee, to hear Pastor J. Konrad Hölé speak. Hölé, who I had never met before, was known to move in the prophetic. Arriving early, I was invited by my friend Mike, the pastor of the church, to visit with him and J. Konrad in the parsonage prior to the service. The three of us were sitting there in the living room talking when out of nowhere J. Konrad looks at me and says, "God has called you to be an apostle." I looked at him thinking, *I'm just barely making it as a pastor. I don't have a clue what it means to be an apostle. Aren't those the guys who wrote the New Testament? The ones who were beaten, persecuted, stoned, run out of town, and usually died as martyrs? I don't think I'm interested.*

It's true I did a lot of exciting things growing up. My dad loved adventure. He was an aerospace engineer and later a construction superintendent. Our family lived all over the place, from Seattle, Washington, to Bartow, Florida. We never lived anywhere for more than two years. In fact, during my eighth through twelfth grade years, our home consisted of a camper and travel trailer.

Every weekend was an adventure. As soon as Dad got off work, we would hit the road. One weekend we would be at the beach, surfing and scuba diving. Another weekend we would be hiking to the top of a 14,000-foot mountain. Another we would be riding dirt bikes in the desert and then later at a local motocross track in town. Yet another would find us water-skiing on a river. I never became an expert at any of those activities, but pretty good at all of them just the same. At the time, I didn't consider as I do now that the mark of an apostle is to be a jack of all trades and a master of none.

I was born in 1959 and by the time 1989 rolled around, I had played high school football; ridden a bicycle across America; competed in triathlons; raced a motorcycle in the Houston Astrodome, New Orleans Superdome, and Atlanta Stadium; and had a room full of trophies. I fished for sharks in the ocean out of a canoe, surfed in hurricanes, wind surfed, and barefoot water-skied. Yet something was missing.

I remember being on the boardwalk in Atlantic City in 1986, having just finished a 3,000-mile bicycle trip in six weeks and four days. I had thought the cross-country trek would satisfy a drive inside of me and take away the emptiness. Guess what. It was a great experience, but I was still empty.

I boarded a plane and flew to Memphis where my wife Denise picked me up and drove me to Forest City, Arkansas, so I could compete in a triathlon. I didn't even bother going home for a break after the long cycle ride across America. I placed thirty-third out of five hundred in the triathlon. But I was still empty.

My parents had been raised in church. They met when they were only twelve years old. Neither of them dated another person. They got married when they were twenty and had me a year later. Although they quit going to church while I was still young, the basic principles of Christianity stayed with us. Those principles and our staying busy kept me out of a lot of trouble. Besides, my dad was six feet, two hundred twenty pounds and knew how to use a belt. Fear kept me out of a lot of trouble—the sort of fear that could probably help some of our youth today.

I first met Denise at a motorcycle race in 1980. We began dating in 1982 and were married within the year. Denise grew up in Counce, Tennessee. When I first came to know her, she was living at the same house she always had been. Talk about a couple—her having always lived at the same place and me never staying anywhere for very long.

In 1983 the two of us became foster parents. Over the next ten years we would see over a hundred children come through our home. We wound up adopting three of them. God was setting us up.

In 1988 Denise gave birth to a daughter. By then my father-in-law had managed to get me a job at the local paper mill. Good money. Good benefits. I should have been satisfied. After all, I had traveled the U.S., participated in many sports, was healthy, had a beautiful wife and children, and now a good job. But something was still missing. That, however, was about to change.

The job at the paper mill made it possible for Denise and me to buy a nice house right next to the First Baptist Church down the street from where my mother-in-law lived. Denise had grown up in that church. Her mother had been a member there forever. After moving into our new home, Denise began taking the kids to that church. I got to thinking, *My grandparents used to take me. It wasn't that bad.* Being concerned with how to deal with all the foster children coming through our home, I figured church might help me provide them with some answers. I believed that the Bible was God's book even though I hadn't read much of it. I knew a lot of people had opinions about how we should live, but I figured if we always went back to God's ways, things should work out. What I didn't count on was God doing more than simply teach me some new ways about things, let alone give me a new life. I didn't know I would end up finding the one person who could fill that empty spot in me that nothing else could satisfy.

William, a friend of mine at the paper mill, encouraged me to come to the Sunday school class he taught at the church. So I did. Who knows how God moves. One thing I did know is that William had a heart for souls. Little did either of us know that destiny would strike one February night in 1989.

A maintenance man at the mill, William was given a work order to change a gasket in a pipe that night, unaware that the line was plugged with chips full of caustic acid, under pressure, and extremely hot. No sooner had he loosened the pipe when, without warning, the line blew open, knocking his hard hat clean off his head and covering him in acid. At the time, I happened to be in the shop getting supplies. William came running in screaming as though he was under attack by a swarm of hornets. The caustic had eaten right through his insulated clothing.

A number of men quickly gathered around him, stripped off his clothing, and began washing him in vinegar to neutralize the acid. Despite their valiant efforts, within moments all of the hair on William's head had been eaten off, skin was hanging from his arms and other parts of his body, and his eyes were but a white glaze. His pupils could not be seen. It was almost like something out of a horror movie, only this was real life. And I was right there watching the whole thing while trying to help.

I noticed that as soon as the men got around William, he quickly began to calm down. It was amazing. Maybe he had been in shock, but as I look back on that night it's obvious God's hand was upon him. I can still see the men rushing to get William to the hospital. At the time, it shook me up. It caused me to ask, *Would God allow this to happen?* Maybe it had been allowed to shake me up … to make me think.

Now, I know this will mess with the theology of some who think that God only allows good things to happen to people, but William's tragedy caused communities to come together and pray, and it alleviated some stress between management and union workers at the paper mill. Later, William would visit many churches to testify of the goodness of God.

So, why is it so many people act as if suffering is a sign of failure when it's in the midst of suffering that we find out what we're really made of. It's easy to pray and serve God when all heaven is coming down, but what about when all hell is breaking loose. Imagine lying in a hospital room where every day someone comes in to scrape off newly formed scabs from your body so you won't become infected, all the while unable to see anything, not knowing what the future holds, knowing only *who* holds it, just as William experienced. And what if death comes?

The Bible talks about a man named Stephen, full of faith and the Holy Spirit, being stoned to death while a religious leader named Saul stood by giving his approval, thinking he was doing God a favor. Later, a man of God named James was put to death by the sword at the order of King Herod who, when he saw that it pleased religious folk to mistreat the followers of Jesus, had the apostle Peter caught and locked up in prison. However, on the very night that Herod was going to bring Peter before the people to condemn him, an angel delivered him from not one, not two, not three, but four squads of soldiers! James' death drove people to intensive prayer, delivering Peter from his death.

It's a risk to tell God, "Do whatever you want to do with me." There are no guarantees of safety or easy journeys. The early apostles faced this sort of uncertainty on a regular basis. Yet, they placed their lives in the hand of the Master who knows all things.

Not long after Saul approved of Stephen's death, he had a life-changing encounter. In Acts 9 we read that while he was on the way to Damascus to take prisoner those who believed in Jesus, suddenly a light from heaven shone around him and he fell to the ground. The glory of the Lord had struck him in such a way that he could not stand. The Lord then spoke to him. Other men who were with him also heard the Lord's voice but saw no one. Jesus revealed to Saul that when he persecuted those who believed in Him, he was actually persecuting the Lord Himself. Trembling, Saul asked Jesus what he should do. In response, the Lord gave him his first instruction: "... get up and enter the city, and it will be told you what you must do" (verse 6).

When Saul got up from the ground, he could not see and had to be led into town by hand. He remained blind for three days and didn't eat or drink. The Lord then gave a disciple named Ananias specific instruction on where to find Saul and to lay hands on him so that he would not only regain his sight but be filled with the Holy Spirit! The Lord likewise showed Saul a vision of Ananias coming in to the home where he was and laying hands on him. Both men received instruction and revelation from the Lord. Both obeyed. Both received confirmation on what the Lord had shown them.

Saul, who would later be known as Paul, was now sold out for Jesus. Thank God that after becoming a believer he didn't just hang out but went on to Do The Stuff (preach the gospel of the kingdom, heal the sick, cleanse the lepers, raise the dead, cast out demons) and even write a large portion of the New Testament. As a chosen vessel of God, Paul allowed the Lord to use him in whatever way He wanted.

Of the first twelve apostles, it is believed that at least ten suffered martyrdom. There is a saying: "The blood of the martyrs is the seed of revival." A problem in the church today is that many would-be apostles want the title without the risk. Many expect four-star motels, lavish food, and red-carpet superstar status. It's just the excuse modern-day theologians need to point to in asserting that apostles aren't for today, that they were only for the early church. I'll speak more on this later.

About a week after William's admittance to the hospital, I

called to see how he was doing. I was told he had severe burns and skin transplants, and that he was blind. William would later say, "I always prayed for a powerful testimony like others had." Well, he got it. In time, William would regain some of his sight and most of his health, but he would never work at the paper mill again.

The thing is, if you hadn't seen William after the accident and had only talked to him over the phone, you wouldn't have known that he had been in an accident. There was such a peace in his heart. Meanwhile, fear began to invade my heart. *What if this happened to me? Would I have the peace that William had? What if I was blinded overnight, lost my job, spent many months in pain, and couldn't drive again? Would I survive that? Would I have peace?* I didn't have peace as it was. William had something I didn't, and the desire for that something was beginning to invade my soul. It was what I had been looking for—not simply learning some Bible stories or about a better way of life, but a transformation. God's plan was coming about.

I don't remember what our pastor preached about one Sunday morning after that, but thank God it was a church with altar calls. That morning, I would leave my pew, take a short walk to the altar, and say a simple prayer that would change my life forever: "Lord, I'm a sinner and I need to be saved."

I didn't weep or cry or get real emotional, but I'm here to tell you that something happened. The Bible says that if anyone is in Christ, he is a new creation; that the old things have passed away and all things have become new (see 2 Corinthians 5:17). I had been delivered from darkness and brought into the Light.

In my eyes, I hadn't been a bad person; but one doesn't have to be bad to miss the mark with God. It's not about how we see ourselves; it's about how God sees us. The apostle Paul said, "… all have sinned and fall short of the glory of God" (Romans 3:23). The good news is that while the wages of sin is death, the gift of God is eternal life in Christ Jesus our Lord! (See

Romans 6:23.) The Bible says, "WHOEVER WILL CALL ON THE NAME OF THE LORD WILL BE SAVED" (Romans 10:13).

I had become a new man. Jesus had filled the emptiness inside of me that only He could fill. The real journey had begun. And even now, more than twenty years later, He's still filling me!

Maybe you've experienced something similar. You're a good person but empty. Listen, only Jesus can give you real life. God's book says that "if you confess with your mouth Jesus as Lord, and believe in your heart that God raised Him from the dead, you will be saved" (Romans 10:9). If you're feeling empty and missing that something, why don't you do what I did: bow your head and cry out to God, "Lord, I'm a sinner and I need to be saved!"

I guarantee you, it will change the rest of your life.

2

Holy Ghost

It was midnight. I was standing in the parking lot of the Freewill Baptist Church with my hands in the air. The air felt like it was full of electricity. The hair on my arms stood up. From the top of my head to the bottom of my feet it felt as though an electric current was flowing through my body. *What is going on?* I wondered. I had never felt anything like it before. I had simply been listening to a man preach about the New Age Movement and nothing was even said about the Holy Spirit. I thought somehow they had plugged my pew into an electrical outlet. It had come on so strong that I was getting goose bumps.

I waited until the service ended and everyone else had left before I caught up with the preacher in the parking lot. We spent an hour talking about the Holy Spirit while his wife and kids waited in the car. The preacher, Tim Carothers, said to me, "Brother Bill, God wants to fill you with the Holy Spirit. Could I pray for you?" He laid his hands on me and began to pray for God to baptize me in the Holy Spirit.

I had heard about a baptism in the Holy Spirit from some friends at the paper mill. They had been telling me, "Bill, we know you are saved, but there is more." *What do you mean, "more"?* I thought. I had given my life to Jesus. I was a new man. My family was changing. Jesus had filled that empty spot inside of me. I had spoken at Sunday morning services at the local state park. I had been water baptized. The church voted me in as deacon only eight months after my salvation. I thought I was on my way.

My friends at the mill told me that although I had the Holy Spirit, God wanted to pour out His Spirit upon me so that I would have power to Do The Stuff that the Bible talks about. There seemed to be something different about these guys. They were "Pentecostal" ... "Full Gospel" ... "Charismatic" ... something. Everything they said to me sounded okay until they told me that when Jesus baptized me in the Holy Ghost, I would speak in other tongues. Now that was crossing the line. I thought, *Why would I need to speak in tongues?* It sounded pretty foolish to me. Although, I had read about it in the Book of Acts. It happened at the beginning of the church. It was how the church started.

My pastor, who lived next door to me, had told me to read the Book of Acts. He had given me a paperback New Testament Bible. After reading the first four books (Matthew, Mark, Luke, and John), I went to his house to ask him a question: "Are all the books in the Bible the same stories about Jesus?" "No," he said. "The next book is the Book of Acts and is talking about the beginning of the church."

I think he may have gotten excited and told the church that I should be made a deacon because I was actually reading the book. I say, be careful if you start reading the Bible because things will begin to happen. There is more.

As I stood there in the parking lot of that Baptist church with my hands lifted up, I could feel God's presence all over me. I wasn't speaking in tongues, though I could feel His power. After praying for me, the preacher said, "Within three days you will be speaking in tongues." Those words were kind of scary to me. I wondered if he was just saying that or if it was actually true. I knew I couldn't make it happen, and that he couldn't make it happen, for if we could have, it would have. But God had a plan. It was now after midnight. I was tired. And I was sure the preacher was tired. So we went our separate ways.

Jesus was in the process of empowering me. I was saved but was about to be filled. The door was about to be opened into the Spirit realm. In the Book of Acts it says, "…you will receive power when the Holy Spirit has come upon you…" (1:8). It was that power I would need to Do The Stuff. We must be filled with the Spirit to go where the natural mind cannot go.

Our natural minds cannot figure out a prophetic word that has been given for somebody we know nothing about. Our natural minds cannot figure out the gift of miracles when a man on oxygen and confined to a wheelchair takes the oxygen mask off, gets out of the wheelchair, and is made whole. Our natural minds cannot understand how one person can give a message in tongues and another interpret it, the message being given not only for a particular lost soul from another country, but provided in that person's native language and with proper interpretation, confirming that Jesus is the Son of God and the only way to heaven. Oh, don't get me to preaching now. Do you see why we need that spiritual door open? It was coming to me soon.

I was up at about eight o'clock the following morning, still feeling good. My wife had taken our kids to school. It was the Monday of a long weekend. I was in the bedroom when I opened my Bible and began reading in the Book of John. I don't remember exactly where in the book I was reading, but all of a sudden someone came in the room. He didn't knock at the door; He just filled the whole room. I couldn't see Him, but the Holy Spirit was there even more tangibly than the previous night. I began to weep in His presence which was stronger than I had ever felt before. As I wept, all of a sudden I began speaking in other tongues just as the first apostles did in the Book of Acts. It felt like God had taken the top of my head off and poured rocket fuel down inside of me.

As I continued to speak in this new language, a voice came to me saying, "You need to shut up! You don't know how stupid you sound." Well, it may have sounded stupid, but it sure felt good. God was filling me with His Spirit. Jesus once said to a Jewish ruler named Nicodemus, "Truly, truly, I say to you, unless one is born again he cannot see the kingdom of God ... unless one is born of water and the Spirit he cannot enter into the kingdom of God" (John 3:3, 5).

The door had just opened and I entered into His kingdom, the kingdom of Heaven. I just walked right into the Spirit realm. It was awesome. For the next two weeks it was as if I was walking on air. I was singing a new song and speaking in a new prayer language that went directly to my heavenly Father. The Bible was coming alive like never before.

It wasn't long before I sold a Ruger .44 Magnum that I had kept near my bed. I used the money to buy my wife a sewing machine. Now, you know you have the Holy Ghost when you sell your pistol to buy your wife a sewing machine. I had that gun for protection. If anyone had broken into our home, all I would have had to do was fire one shot and they'd be gone. With a .44 Magnum, you wouldn't necessarily need to hit an intruder; just the sound of it going off would scare most people away. But I realized that gun was just a pea shooter to what I had now. The One who created the earth, the stars, the moon and the sun, called them by name and flung them into orbit, was now living inside of me. The same Spirit that raised Jesus from the dead was living inside of me! If someone attacked me now, they would have to deal with God, the One living inside of me, as well as great big angels encamped round about me. No weapon formed against me will prosper!

The Bible says you shall receive power when the Holy Ghost comes upon you, and that's what I had now. I've been in inner cities and lived on reservations, and have not carried a gun for protection since that day the Holy Spirit invaded my bedroom many years ago. I only had one remaining fear: *How am I going to tell my wife?*

Denise had been raised in the Baptist church where it was taught that speaking in tongues is of the devil. It had been about two weeks. I was on my way home from an evening shift at the paper mill, floating in the glory. At work, I would sing songs and hymns and spiritual songs while unloading railroad cars full of coal. It was awesome. I had told my Pentecostal friends, "I'm sorry, you're right. There *is* more. I got Him." But now it was time to tell my wife. So I told God on the way home that evening, "If our kids are in bed and my wife is still up, I'll talk to her tonight."

When I got home, the kids were in bed and the wife was still up. I tried to ask God for another night, but that was His appointed night for me to come clean. So I said to Denise, "Sweetie, let's talk." We sat down on the couch together. I asked her, "Are you sure you're saved?"

Whew! I almost had to duck. She said, "Yes, I'm saved!" Now remember, after we became married, it was she who started going back to church and taking the kids with her. I didn't start going until later. I hadn't asked her the question since being saved for about a year and was now asking it after having been baptized in the Holy Spirit for two weeks. Jesus told his disciples that He would give them power to be his witnesses, even to the end of the earth! For the moment, all I needed was power to deal with what was going on in my living room.

Family members can be the hardest ones to witness to sometimes. But I now had the power to talk. And I asked the question. My wife answered the question. But what she said next I wasn't prepared for. She said, "I want to ask you a question. What has happened to you in the past two weeks?" She realized there was something different about me even though I hadn't said a word about it.

The Holy Ghost is awesome. This was not a theological debate. The proof was in the pudding, as they say. Denise had been noticing a transformation during those two weeks, even though I had been saved for a year. So I began to tell her what happened to me at the Freewill Baptist Church that one night. Her eyes got big like a deer in the headlights. After all, she had heard about speaking in tongues. And now she was married to a tongue-talker? Oh, my gosh! She said, "Well, I know something happened to you, but I don't think I'm ready for that yet."

Fast-forward to a year later. Once, while at a deacons meeting, I felt rather ill. I asked those in attendance to anoint me with oil and pray for me according to what it says in James 5:14: "Is anyone among you sick? Then he must call for the elders of the church and they are to pray over him, anointing him with oil in the name of the Lord." They said they didn't have any oil. Well, I just happened to have some. So they anointed me with the oil and prayed for me. I felt better afterwards.

After the evening service that night, the pastor called a special deacons meeting. It was about the oil. He told me they didn't do that in this church. He said that's how cults get started and it's not what the scripture meant. He said the scripture meant that you call the elders and they see if you're sick enough to need a doctor and some medicine. He said the oil represents medicine.

That blew me away. I had already told him about my speaking in tongues. Since I didn't want to cause any problems, I resigned all of my positions from the church. Denise and I then began attending a fellowship called Church on the Rock.

Nobody told me there were parts of the Bible that were not for today, as if in the beginning powerful things happened among a certain group of people, then faded away and were no longer needed. Even before I had been saved, I believed the Bible was God's Word and that it was true from front to back.

I would come to find out that there are liberal and conservative believers; those who think some of the Bible is truth with some stories mixed in for our teaching, and those who believe the entire Bible is God's word and all truth. But even among conservative believers, I found there were those who believed that the sort of things that happened in the Book of Acts ceased to continue after the first apostles died.

One day, I was reading in the first chapter of the Book of Mark about Jesus casting an unclean spirit out of a man. I went and asked our pastor, "When are we going to cast devils out?" He told me there are no demons today. He said that in the days of Jesus they didn't know the names of certain sicknesses and so they referred to them as demons, but that we now know the names of the sicknesses.

I thought to myself that it would be strange if Jesus, the only begotten Son of the all-knowing, all-present, all-powerful, one true God, did not know the names of certain illnesses and referred to them as demons instead. That just didn't make sense. The Bible says that Jesus cast out demons and that He healed the sick. I think He knew the difference between demons and illnesses.

Something else I considered to be really strange is that a lot of people who refer to themselves as "Full Gospel" believe that Jesus gave to the church evangelists, pastors and teachers, but stopped giving apostles and prophets. How can we take five *offices* appearing in the very same Bible verse and say that three are for today but the other two aren't? Now, I'm not a theologian, but something is a little strange here. We are living in a day and time when we need every gift of the Holy Spirit and every gift of Jesus.

I believe what it says about Jesus in Acts 3:21: "whom heaven must receive until the period of restoration of all things about which God spoke by the mouth of His holy prophets from ancient time." Again, I am not a theologian, but my interpretation here is that heaven must keep Jesus until the restoration; that is, a return to a perfect state of being as in the time of Adam before the fall.

The Bible says, "And He gave some as apostles, and some as prophets, and some as evangelists, and some as pastors and teachers … until we all attain to the unity of the faith, and of the knowledge of the Son of God, to a mature man, to the measure of the stature which belongs to the fullness of Christ" (Ephesians 4:11, 13). The purpose of this "five-fold ministry," as it's called, is to equip the saints for the work of the ministry until we become the mature men and women of Christ that God wants us to be; a glorious church, the spotless bride that Christ died and shed his blood to purify; rather than a church that is beaten up, beaten down, and hiding out in a closet or waiting for a rescue mission from heaven to get her out of this place before she perishes.

We are to be the light of the world, the salt of the earth, the hope of those who are suffering. We are the cure for the sicknesses of the world. We are here until we become like Him; until the Church is manifesting His presence. All creation is waiting for the manifest presence of the sons of God and we are it! That time of the restoration of all things is getting closer all the time.

I had been called by God to preach on October 31, 1991, and was later ordained and made a board member at Church on the Rock. While at the Rock, Denise and I, along with a few other couples, took a mission trip to Saltillo, Mexico. While in a morning devotion, during a time of worship and prayer, Jesus baptized my wife in the Holy Ghost … with the evidence of speaking in tongues! Praise God. I said, "Sweetie, if you'd gotten filled in Tennessee, we wouldn't have had to drive a thousand miles for you to be filled in Mexico." God has a sense of humor.

You know what though? No matter how far you have to drive or fly, or how many times you have to go to the altar and pray, or how often you have to ask God to fill you with the Holy Spirit, you need to keep going after Him until He does. It's His desire for all to be filled. Acts 2:39 says, "For the promise is unto you, and to your children, and to all that are afar off, even as many as the Lord our God shall call" (KJV). Just pray and ask God to fill you with the Holy Ghost and to baptize you in His power. On this journey, the only way you'll connect in the Spirit realm and get beyond your natural mind is for God to fill you with the Holy Spirit. It's the door into the Spirit realm.

And don't stop there like many people who speak in tongues one day and think that's it. I'm here to tell you that's not just it. You don't want to stop right there. That's just the door beginning to open. You need to go inside the Kingdom of God. You need to press into the things of the Spirit. The Bible says that when you pray in tongues, you edify yourself. I believe that's how you build yourself up in the power of God. The apostle Paul said, "One who speaks in a tongue edifies himself; but one who prophesies edifies the church" (1 Corinthians 14:4). Prophecy is edification, exhortation, and comfort to men. How are you going to comfort men if you've not been comforted yourself? How are you going to edify others if you yourself have not been built up? How are you going to give away something you don't have? The only way you can get that something is to pray in the Spirit. The Book of Jude says that when we pray in the Spirit, we build up our "most holy faith" (verse 20).

So, we have to pray to build up our faith. It's like a battery. If you let a battery just sit on a shelf, eventually it will be no good. But if it's charged, discharged, and recharged, it will last longer. You have to get charged up if you're going to give anything away to other people. When you pray in the Spirit, you're charging your battery … you're building up that spirit … you're building up that power to be a witness. So, just keep praying in the Spirit, asking God to fill you with His Spirit, and eventually things will begin to flow out; the gifts of the Spirit will come. A word of wisdom. A word of knowledge. A prophetic word. A gift of miracles. A gift of healing. Discernment. Speaking in tongues. Interpretations.

The key that opens the door is baptism in the Holy Spirit. You must ask God to fill you with the Holy Spirit. Then you can begin to operate in the things of the Spirit. You can pray for the sick without being baptized in the Holy Spirit, but I'm here to tell you that you will be a lot more effective if you're filled with the Spirit.

Something happened when God filled me with His Spirit. Something came alive inside of me. I wanted to cast out demons and I wanted to lay hands on the sick; something that didn't seem to be alive before. So, in this journey, in this mission that God has called us to, we need to be filled with the Spirit. We need to be saved, to be baptized in water, and to ask Jesus to baptize us in the Holy Ghost.

In the Book of Acts, Chapter 1, we read that before Jesus sent his disciples out into the world, He spoke to them "of the things pertaining to the kingdom of God" (verse 3 KJV). As He was about to be taken up into heaven, Jesus basically told his disciples to not go out and preach right away — like, to not get any radio or TV shows, or pass out flyers — but to simply wait for "the promise of the Father" which they had heard from Him (verse 4).

Think about it. The disciples of Jesus had been with Him for three and a half years. They had the Word of God made flesh, dwelling among them, preaching and ministering to them. And yet, that wasn't enough. Jesus told them they needed to wait until they received the baptism of the Holy Spirit; then they would be ready to go. If they needed it back then, WHY WOULDN'T WE NEED IT TODAY? I plead with you, be baptized in the Holy Ghost if you want to fulfill everything God has for you. Hallelujah! In Jesus' name.

In the 1500s, Martin Luther had the revelation of being saved by faith rather than by works. We take that for granted now, but back then it was a revelation that caused a revolution.

In the 1700s, the Moravians had a revelation of worship and prayer that brought in God's presence and launched a world-wide mission movement that saw one hundred full-time missionaries sent out over the course of twenty years. One of these missionaries would share his faith with a soul-searching man by the name of John Wesley who, after being saved, brought nations into revival.

In the 1800s, there was revival in Cane Ridge, Kentucky, in which people swooned and were "slain" in the Spirit. There were strange manifestations of God's presence. There was revelation that God was the Healer.

In 1901, there was a revelation at Charles Parham's Bethel Bible College in Topeka, Kansas, that evidence of the baptism in the Holy Spirit is speaking in tongues. Such evidence had manifested all throughout history but was not really linked as evidence until this point in time. It would be the century of the Pentecostal movement beginning with the Azusa Street Revival in 1906.

The Great Healing movements from 1946 to 1964, and the Latter Rain movement in the 60s and 70s, were times when many in traditional churches were baptized in the Holy Spirit and had the experience of speaking in tongues. Various gifts of the Spirit also began to flow during that time. In the 1970s and 80s there was revelation about the restoration of the prophets.

The Bible says that faith comes by hearing, and hearing by the word of God (see Romans 10:17). As we begin to get revelation and preach from the Word of God, the revelations begin to manifest. There are always growing pains and learning curves as God begins to reveal truth to us. We are being stretched. Many people point to mistakes and failures of past movements as the reason for why there are false movements and false prophets today and why the prophetic gift is not for today. I believe that because men and women of God continued proclaiming that God was raising up prophets, regardless of opposition, we do have prophets in the land today.

I am sure that in the 1950s, 60s, and 70s you could have gone into a Christian bookstore and found it hard to locate a single book on prophets or prophetic movements. But in the late

80s and 90s there were prophetic conferences, prophetic movements, and prophetic books as many men and women began to realize there were prophets—a gift of Jesus Christ—given to the Church. God was restoring things.

One of the things that modern-day prophets were proclaiming was great revival. They foresaw people moving in the power of God. They saw restoration of apostles; men and women of God—*sent ones*—who would flow in the power of God and impart that power to others to reach a lost and dying world for Jesus Christ and bring glory to His name. I believe the restoration of the apostles and prophets is something that has to happen before Christ will come again.

So praise God, I had now received the promise of the Holy Ghost. I had been endued with power from on high. But where would I go from here?

The Lord had me on a journey. And it was time to kill the pigs!

3

Getting The Pigs Out

December 1996. I was performing my first wedding. An outdoor wedding with 1,500 to 2,000 people in attendance. God had provided the music and someone to videotape the service and — oh, I almost forgot to tell you, it was on the front steps of the Brownsville Revival. The wedding guests were those who had been standing in line all day to get in that night.

The couple just all of a sudden decided to get married after coming down with our church group on a bus trip from Bolivar. We had known them for only about two weeks. I wasn't aware they had been living together for seven years. During the altar call the previous night, the two ran to the altar and gave their lives to Jesus. And now they wanted to make things right with God.

A couple of key traits of apostles, I believe, are adaptability and flexibility. I wanted to do the wedding when we got back to Tennessee, but the couple wanted to be married right away. I had never married anyone before and didn't have my little black book with the ceremony in it. I'd hardly even seen a wedding. The only weddings I had ever been to were my own and one or two others.

Yet, God had provided the couple money for a marriage license and a driver to take them to the courthouse to get that license. So there I was, sitting in someone's van, sweating and praying, trying to figure out how I was going to do the ceremony ... or come up with a good excuse not to. The couple had asked the ushers at Brownsville for permission to be married on the front steps before the doors opened that night and it was granted to them. One of the "guests" had sung on the Trinity Broadcasting Network and offered to do a wedding song for them. Another man with a video camera offered to film the entire service. It was a done deal. Man, did God stretch me that day. And all I wanted to do was enjoy revival.

Only the day before, while assigning people in our group to motel rooms, I was going to give the couple their own room. I thought, *You know, they had just been in our church about two weeks. Put them in a nice room by themselves.* As the man and I were walking over to the motel office to sort out some of the keys, I asked him how long they had been married. He said, "We're not married. We've been living together for seven years." I immediately thought, *Oh my goodness, I can't do this. We're on a church trip!* So, I had to change everyone's room assignment to get men together with men, and women together with women, assigning the two engaged individuals to separate rooms for the time we were there. No compromise at revival. I didn't care how long the couple had been living together; I wasn't about to give them their own private room. It would have been easy to do without anyone else knowing about their situation, but be assured that your compromise will always find you out. The couple were not offended and were willing to do whatever was right in the eyes of God. By the end of the afternoon, I had performed my first wedding. And with a whole lot of people watching!

I had made my first trip down to this revival nine months earlier after hearing about it from some friends who had gone before. I said, "I'm gonna go." Revival is work, but it's worth it.

My goal was to see the people in my church have a radical encounter with the living God. And whatever it took, I would do. I had recently joined the Assemblies of God and was pastoring my first church. We even started a Christian school. I didn't know a lot about pastoring, but I was hungry for God. So, one day in April 1996, I loaded up my four kids and off we went to Florida for a little vacation. Beach by day, revival by night. You couldn't beat that. Arriving in Pensacola, we got a motel room a few miles east of the church. I didn't know what I was in for.

We went to the beach and then to church, showing up at around 6:00 PM. Back then, you didn't have to stand in line. I had heard that after the regular altar call each night, people would lay hands on you and pray, "More, Lord." Somehow, we wound up in a front row pew — maybe because I was a pastor and they had some special seating for pastors. But this I knew: the presence of God was strong in that place. I'm getting messed up just writing this. And after all these years. Whew!

I had told my kids, "After the altar call, I don't want to see you guys talking, walking around, or going to the bathroom. You better be finding one of those people with a badge on and have them lay hands on you. We need more of God and we need this at our church." I was serious. They must have taken me at my word, because they did just what I told them to do.

That night, the worship was great and the preaching was powerful, but the altar call just blew me away. There I was, standing right in the front row, next to an aisle, when this guy comes running by me, hits his knees, and slides into the altar. Wow! Others followed, one after another, until several hundred people were up front praying, asking Jesus into their lives, repenting of their sins, being restored in their walk with God.

Then came time for individual prayer ... for more of God. The church had special prayer teams trained to lay hands on people and pray for them. They would simply touch your head or hands and pray for more of the Lord in your life. The pastors and some of the ministers who were on the platform would also walk around praying for people, releasing impartations. When that time for more prayer came, the kids and I went our separate ways seeking prayer. If I was going to tell my kids to get prayer, you can be assured I was going to get it too; and not just one prayer, but as many as I could get before they turned the lights off and ran us out of the building.

Each prayer was like a drink of heavenly wine. You could sense the presence of God coming on — kind of like a buzz coming on. It's amazing how some people would travel long distances to get to revival and either stand and watch or only get prayed for one time. I don't know if they thought it was foolish or what. But there was an impartation that would come upon you as you were being prayed for ... and it was transferrable! You could become a carrier of something you didn't have thirty minutes earlier. I was already baptized in the Holy Spirit, but this was different.

The best way I can describe what it felt like while being prayed for is this: it's like sitting in a chair at the dentist's office and they put the clown nose or mask over your face, then turn the valve to release the nitrous into your system before they deaden your nerves by giving you shots. That's what it was like for me. Some people call it laughing gas. Whew! You feel like, *Just go ahead and cut my head off. I don't care.* You can feel the gas going down through your body as it gets into your blood system and flows down into your arms and legs. You begin to tingle all over as if by a light voltage of electricity. That's what it can feel like when people begin to pray for you. You begin to get that tingly feeling from the top of your head down throughout your entire body. Sometimes, different body parts go almost numb and you can't move them. Sometimes, you can't walk for a while. You might not even be able to talk. It's like you're being possessed by another spirit; the Holy Spirit. If people can be possessed by demonic spirits, why can't we be possessed by the Holy Spirit.

At the time I wondered, *What is this new level of God's*

presence? I have been in revivals before. I have been prayed for. I have been prophesied over. But something different is going on here. It was another level of God's anointing, but what.

It wasn't long before they started blinking the lights on and off. It was about midnight and time for us to get out of the place so they could clean it up and get ready for the next day. After I got up off the floor, I started looking around for my children. A lot of people had cleared out already. I spotted one of my kids under a front pew, her hair all messed up, looking all strange. Another was about twelve rows back in an aisle, walking around looking kind of lost. Another was at the altar. I then heard someone shouting or screaming. I looked over and saw about twenty people gathered around my oldest daughter as she said, "He spoke to me. He spoke to me." She had heard the Lord's voice as she lay there on the floor under the power of God.

She was kind of like some people mentioned in the Bible who had an encounter with God. She couldn't walk. In fact, she could hardly move. An usher told me to get my van and pull it around to the side door. They would load my daughter in a wheelchair and meet me over there. It worked out well because at the time, I had a Ford Aerostar with no rear seat. We just opened the rear hatch and rolled her right in. The other three kids jumped in behind. They were jerking and bobbing and shaking under the power of God. Man, talk about a van load of weirdos!

We stopped at Papa John's on the way back to the motel. I said to the kids, "Stay in the van, and I'll go in and order the pizza." Despite being under a heavy influence of the Spirit, I remained pretty dignified and was able to contain myself. I ordered the pizzas and was standing there waiting when I heard the bell on the door jingle. I looked over. In walked the kids. One was doing something of a chicken walk. Another was jerking. Another was making funny bird noises like, "Whouuw!" You should've seen the look on the pizza guy's face. My dignity left me. I was thinking, *What are you guys doing? I thought I told you to stay in the car.* But I could sense God saying, "I'm going to help you be a witness." So I started to explain to the guy what was happening and invited him to go to the revival. I don't know if he ever did, but I know my kids wouldn't have done what they did on purpose. God has a way for you to be a witness even if you don't want to be. Drunk people do strange things. Drunk in the Spirit, that is.

People drunk on alcohol will get in the middle of the street, take off their clothes, and sing to cars passing by. Yet, the same people get saved, sobered up, and find it hard to talk to anyone about Jesus. That's why we need to be filled.

One hundred and twenty got filled in the upper room on the day of Pentecost. Peter, a disciple of Jesus who had previously denied Him, came out preaching. People standing around outside thought the one hundred and twenty were drunk. And well, they were ... in the Spirit. It's time for Christians to start drinking of the Spirit again. Drunk people will say or do almost anything, anywhere, anytime. We need to be so full of the Spirit that we lose our fear of man and begin to fear God and obey Him. My kids had no fear or shame. It was awesome.

Upon returning to our motel room, the kids and I ate our pizza and then went to sleep — three girls in one bed, my son and I in the other. At about 3:00 AM, I woke up. The bed was shaking. It was almost like one of those old motel room beds some of you may remember where you put a quarter in a slot and it vibrates. *What is this?* I wondered. I looked over at my son. He was shaking under the power of God even though he was asleep. As he lay there and shook, all of a sudden what was happening to him got on me and I began to shake. Eventually, he stopped shaking ... and without ever waking up.

It wasn't long before conviction came upon me. I don't remember anything specific. I was not purposely living in sin. But I knew there was a holiness about what was happening. I got down beside that bed at 3:30 AM and began to repent. I said,

"God, if there is anything in my life that would quench your Spirit or stop me from having more of You, take it away right now. I want to be a carrier of this glory. I want Your presence, not only to be in me but on me. Lord, we need this in our church ... in our city ... in our communities ... in our state ... our nation. We need revival. We need an open heaven." Little did I know the trouble that prayer would bring me.

The Bible says that the Light has come into the world, but that men loved darkness rather than the Light because their deeds were evil (see John 3:19). When you pursue His presence at all cost, some people won't like it. The problem is, God brings His light into the church to set people free and it terrifies them. When the light of His glory shows up on the scene, men get real nervous. It begins to expose their evil deeds and how they've been trying to manipulate God and do church according to man's ways.

Like what Bill Johnson, pastor of Bethel Church in Redding, California, said about Peter on the mount of transfiguration. There Peter was with Jesus, Moses and Elijah before him. It wasn't enough for him to simply stand and bask in the presence; he felt he had to do something ... like start a building program. He wanted to build three tabernacles—one for Jesus, one for Moses, and one for Elijah—up there on the mountain. What happened next is that God's glory showed up. Peter, along with two other disciples, became greatly afraid. (See Matthew 17:1-6; also Luke 9:28-34.)

The Light brings division because it shines in our inner being and begins to reveal things in our lives that are not pleasing to God. Those who open their hearts, let the light shine in, and repent of their sins, experience great freedom. After repentance, there are times of refreshing. There is refreshment in the presence of the Lord.

Those who close their eyes [hearts] and refuse to let the Light examine them become irritated, uneasy, critical of others, and suspicious. They try to put out the light at all costs lest their deeds be exposed. They become religious and declare that things are getting out of hand and unbiblical while others open their hearts and begin to find great freedom and joy.

In revival, there may be shouting, running, shaking, or falling as the Spirit of God deals with people and the weight of sin falls off. Revival brings a dividing sword. There is no middle ground in revival. You cannot serve God on Sunday and act like the devil the rest of the week. You cannot fake your way through a revival service when the glory is there. You have to get in, get out, or squeal a lot.

When I read Mark 5:1-20, it seems to me that Jesus wanted to bring an awakening to the country of the Gadarenes (or, Gerasenes). No sooner did the Lord and his disciples land upon shore when a man full of demons that no one could help threw himself at the feet of Jesus. I believe the demoniac was just along for the ride as the demons were driven to bow before the king of the universe Who had just showed up in their territory. The legion of demons possessing the poor man knew who Jesus was. They had to bow before Him. As it is written, "...every knee shall bow to me, and every tongue shall confess to God" (Romans 14:11 KJV). The demons had to worship Jesus; they had no choice.

Man, however, has a choice. We have been given a freedom. Of all the created things on this earth, man is the only one who can say, "I will not worship You." If Jesus commands the water to be calm and the wind to stop, they have to obey. If He commands the trees to wave or be still, they have to obey. If He commands a donkey to speak, it must speak. If He commands a rooster to crow, it has to crow. And yet, He gives man the right to say, "No, I'll do what I want to do."

The legion of demons in the land of the Gadarenes pleaded with Jesus to not send them out of the country. To me, it's as if they were praying, "Please don't send us away. It's not our time." Nearby was a herd of about two thousand pigs.

Now, swine were to be considered "unclean." They were

not to be eaten by God's people or even touched by them. God had given dietary laws to His people for a reason: to keep them healthy. Thus, the Gadarenes had no business raising pigs in the first place.

Some people think Jesus doesn't mind if they do whatever they have to do in order to make a living, whether it be selling alcohol or cigarettes, engaging in pornography, singing secular music, whatever. But I have news for you: when Jesus shows up, the pigs have to go.

Jesus was about to deal with the Gadarenes' pigs by permitting the demons to enter them. No sooner did the evil spirits leave the man and enter the swine then the entire herd ran violently down a steep embankment and into the sea, committing suicide. Instantly, the demoniac was set free and in his right mind.

Of course, after the pig herders saw all of this, it terrified them. I imagine they went back into town telling everyone, "He killed our pigs! He killed our pigs!" When people from the city and around the country went out and saw the one who had been demon-possessed, sitting and clothed and in his right mind, they became afraid. You would think they would have gone back into town saying, "The man who could not be delivered is now delivered! The one who had been running through the tombs and cutting himself and crying has been delivered!" But no, they were more concerned about their economy than they were a man who was bound up like those bound up right now by drugs and alcohol. We're more concerned about having a comfortable life than we are about those who are oppressed and depressed by demonic powers.

After seeing what happened to their pigs, the Gadarene folk pleaded with Jesus to depart from their region. Rather than being excited to see a man made whole, they became worried over the loss of their swine. They didn't want Jesus coming into their territory and getting rid of their pigs.

It's like people who guard their pet sins. They don't mind

getting rid of a few, but they don't want to have to get rid of all of them. But I'm here to tell you, when God shows up in His glory, it's all got to go! Sin cannot stand in the midst of God's glory. The Lord said, "YOU SHALL BE HOLY, FOR I AM HOLY" (1 Peter 1:16).

What I've got to say to you today is this: Let Him kill your pigs. All of them. Let Him utterly destroy all of the pigs that are ruining your life so you may be completely free of sin. I'm telling you, you're missing something if you don't. Do you think holding on to that little pig is safety? That little pet? That short-lived time of pleasure? There is nothing that compares to His presence. Don't turn Him away.

Just think, if the Gadarenes had welcomed Jesus into their city as He had been in others, all would have been healed, set free, delivered, and saved. The frightened Gadarenes serve as an example as to why so many of our churches today are dead. We want to raise our pigs and justify our sins. We don't want God to clean house. So we just go through our religious routine every Sunday declaring, "Come, Holy Spirit," when in reality, we don't want Him to come, because if He did we might not get out of church in time to make it to the buffet. Besides, we don't want to look foolish rolling around on the floor and getting our hair all messed up, or weeping until the mascara runs; but rather, keep things 'decent' and 'in [our] order.' God help us. We don't want to pray and fast and change our ways. We have a form of godliness while denying the power thereof. And while we're keeping God out, our lost family, friends, and neighbors are dying and going to hell.

There are multitudes of sick and demon-oppressed people in our churches because we don't want God to deal with our pigs. And so Jesus gets in the boat and leaves us to our religious, man-pleasing ways. Come on, church. It's time to wake up! It's time to be the light of the world, to let our light shine, to let His glory and His presence come in, to let Him rule and reign in our churches again!

At the end of our four-day-long revival vacation, the kids and I returned home ... changed. We arrived back in Bolivar on a Saturday evening. After dropping the kids off at home, I went down to the church. Having purchased two Brownsville worship CDs (Volumes 1 and 2), I turned on the CD player, put in the two CDs, and began worshipping in the sanctuary. Man, did His presence come into that place. The next thing I knew, I was laid out on the floor. No one had even touched me. No one but God, that is.

Come Sunday morning, I preached like a man from another planet. The congregation looked at me like I was crazy. I was running around, shouting, jumping off the platform, telling everybody we were sinners and needed to get right with God. I believe I scared them pretty badly. They didn't understand what had happened to me and I didn't use much wisdom in explaining it to them. I preached like Steve Hill: "Get right, or you're going to get left. Get the sin out." I condemned a little more than I encouraged. When God changes you and you have a great encounter like I did, you must use wisdom; be wise as a serpent and harmless as a dove.

People did not respond too well to the altar call that morning and we all left a bit discouraged. It can be a problem to have God moving powerfully in your life when others don't understand. It's a shame that, in general, churches have been dead for so long that this generation doesn't know what a move of God looks like. It's time for those who have seen a move of God to rise up and say, "O God, do not forsake me, until I declare Your strength to this generation, Your power to all who are to come" (Psalm 71:18).

Making it through the weekend, I took the following Monday off to rest. Come early Tuesday morning, I was down at the church again getting ready for the morning chapel service of our Christian school. At about 7:30 AM, I put on a Brownsville CD and began worshipping. God's presence soon filled the atmosphere. Students began to arrive. There were about eighteen children in our school at the time. They came right into the sanctuary. Some sat. Some stood. They were all quiet and orderly. They knew something was up. *Somebody* was in the building ... and it wasn't school as usual. Before long, I called them to the front and began praying for them. It was awesome. As the power of God touched them, they would hit the floor, everyone of them. Everyone except for a little girl who had to use the girls' room. But after my daughters went in there and prayed for her, she went down as well, right there in the restroom.

I began using more wisdom now as God did the work. When you're wanting to bring in His presence, there's no routine that's been handed down for you to follow. It's new territory. Oh, it's in the Bible alright, but you may not have revelation of it until you actually begin to move in it. You're treading out into a river that's getting deeper and deeper. And the deeper it gets, the more it feels as though you're going to lose control. It feels as though you're going to drown or crash into some rocks, or that something you're not going to be in control of is going to happen. But the deeper you get, the more God takes control, and the more things really begin to happen.

There were kids who wanted to come to church and pray every night that week. Some parents became angry over their children wanting to be driven to church every night. Some did bring their kids, or drop them off and wait in their vehicles as their children went inside to pray. Some kids had to be carried out when the prayer meeting was over.

It's crazy how some people will pay for their children to attend Christian school because they want them to follow Christ; yet they don't want them to get radical about it. Some would pray, "God, don't call my kids into full-time missions; just keep them away from drugs and alcohol." They don't mind taking them to little league or the bowling alley or the skating rink, but "Why do we have to bring them to church every night?" I became a bit frustrated over this. When the presence of God falls, it usually brings a sword. It's either all in or all out when revival comes. By the end of summer, we would lose a few people at church. I'd wind up firing the school principal. Basically, all hell broke loose.

We measure God's movement in our churches by the presence of people rather than the presence of Him. When you see the ship sinking, will you give into the pressures of men who would say, "See, I told you so"? Will you listen to the naysayers? Or will you surrender all to Him? Will you be a man-pleaser or a God-pleaser? Do you really want more when it will cost you a price? I did. For one day in His courts is better than a thousand elsewhere, and He was still present. I wanted my life to be presence-driven, not people-driven.

By November, things were beginning to take off and people were getting excited again. That's when I decided to make a return trip to the Brownsville Revival. This time, we would take a bus that would carry most of our church. We were few but hungry.

We enjoyed a leisurely drive down with everyone talking about revival. We had watched some of the videos from Brownsville and people were excited about what God might do. In making it to revival, I had the opportunity to perform a wedding in front of a multitude of people—which wouldn't have happened had I given up and caved in—and God moved in an awesome way that night.

The following day, we would load our bus for the trip home as a different people, changed by an encounter with the living God. It was a glory bus all the way home. For ten or so hours we were overcome by His presence. On that bus you could not run or hide because He was there. Ladies were going into intercessions like it says in Romans 8:26: "... the Spirit also helps our weakness; for we do not know how to pray as we should, but the Spirit Himself intercedes for us with groanings too deep for words." People were slain in the spirit—some lying in the aisle,

Journey Into The Apostolic

some beneath seats. People were being baptized in the Spirit and speaking in tongues. Some were delivered and set free. I had never been in anything like that glory bus ride home from the revival.

As soon as we arrived back home, God began to pour out his Spirit into our church. And He continued to do so for the next twenty-five weeks. Lives were changed. People were called into ministry. And oh yes, conflict came; but that's just part of revival.

The journey of an apostle—a man sent out to demonstrate the power of God—is one of conflict. With Peter, Paul, Barnabus, Silas, and others mentioned in the Book of Acts, it was either revival or riot. People would either want to worship them or kill them. There's not much middle ground for an apostle. The conflict, the persecution, the tribulation; it keeps you humble so that when God does move in powerful ways, you will know it's God and not you. You will be crushed and broken so that God may flow freely through you and without you taking any credit.

In Acts 14:8-20 we read about Paul who, in seeing a man crippled from birth but having faith to be healed, commanded the man to stand up straight on his feet. When others saw the man suddenly leap and walk, they presumed Paul and his companion Barnabus to be gods from heaven. When the local temple priest brought oxen and garlands to offer sacrifice with the people, the two apostles quickly tore their clothes and rushed out into the crowd, letting them know they were but men, preaching the gospel, yet scarcely able to restrain the people from sacrificing to them. Later, certain religious men came to town, and having won over the crowds, stoned Paul and dragged him out of the city, presuming him to be dead. However, as disciples stood around him, he simply got up and went right back into town.

Apostles carry an apostolic anointing. Others who walk with them will also carry that anointing. When walking in such power, there must be discipline. Apostles must carry a determination in their spirits, by the Holy Spirit, to never

48

compromise or be ashamed of a move of God or be satisfied with anything else. They will not be satisfied with stale religion and will, at times, bring a holy conflict into the church to get their sails up and catch the wind of the Holy Spirit again. In that pushing is conflict without compromise. Apostles call people to be uncomfortable with the status quo walk with God. Apostles push the church to get out from behind its four walls to win a lost and dying world to Jesus. And apostles will lead the way.

Denominations remove apostles or wait for them to die off so they can build administrations to hold down the fort. They build bank accounts for the future. They put up big buildings and come up with reasons for why they can't afford to go into the entire world. "Because the cost is too great," they say.

How many churches in our nation have no mission-mindedness, no plan to reach the world or local communities, no missions budget? Are we concerned only with the members of our own church? Apostles will cause such a mindset to become very uncomfortable. As such, they will generally not be welcomed.

Only a move of God will change the self-centered, selfish mindset. I believe apostles have a calling to reach the world and that they are given an anointing to explode the church from out of its walls. They have journeys and stories to cause people to become awakened, and with an anointing to launch them out from their church pews into a lost and dying world.

4

Motorcycle Races

My heart pounded as I was about to walk out in front of a hundred and fifty motorcyclists looking like they were ready for combat dressed in boots, helmets, goggles, gloves, special pants, shoulder pads; full protection from head to toe to help avoid injury not only while traversing a course full of trees, rocks, roots, and hills, but in the event of making contact with one or more other riders. In a span of only five minutes, I delivered a short devotion with prayer. I then got on a Suzuki RMX250 ... my heart beating rapidly. It had been about fourteen years since I last rode and I had gotten in only a few days practice before this event. Why would I do this to myself.

I had resigned my position at the church in Bolivar about a year earlier (in 1998). I felt as though I had taken that church as far as I could. Yet, I wasn't sure where to go next. I preached at the church of our presbyter who told me afterwards that the people really enjoyed my message, and that if I should have an interest in being an associate pastor, to let him know. Prior to leaving

Bolivar, one of our church intercessors came to me saying that God told her I had a heart for evangelism and would be leaving the church soon. I wasn't sure which way to go. I knew I needed to feed my family. And Denise and I were in agreement about my working as an associate pastor. So around May I called the presbyter to let him know I was interested. He said it would probably be the end of summer before they could put me on staff.

In the meantime, I decided to volunteer at a youth camp for a week and do some cooking for the kids. I had previously volunteered at camp during my first summer as a pastor, taking with me three youth. At the time, I had never been to a youth camp and thought it would be a nice break. Boy, was I wrong. I was assigned as a team leader to about twenty or thirty kids. They almost killed me. By the fourth day, I had to go to the camp director and ask for mercy. So this time, I volunteered to be a cook. Forget running with the kids.

As the Assemblies of God district office was close to the camp, I thought it would be a good opportunity to visit. So I took off Wednesday of that week to see the superintendent and other leaders. During our conversation, the superintendent told me that the Tennessee district had ten churches without pastors and that I should really pray about taking one of them. That sounded rather exciting to me. Not wanting to wait around, I got the address to one and drove about a hundred miles that night to check it out. It was a big, beautiful church situated on a nice hilltop on ten acres of land. It had a big garage for storing lawn mowers and tractors, and seemed well-equipped. Stepping into the sanctuary, I looked around and imagined it could easily seat about three hundred people. Yet I found only about twelve to fifteen individuals gathered for Bible study that night. Still, I saw a lot of potential in the place. I was excited and just happened to have a resume in my briefcase, so I scheduled a date for me to come and 'try out.'

I called Denise and told her. I don't know how excited she was about going to a new church, but she was excited about the potential for a paycheck. So a couple weeks later we drove up for the Sunday tryout. We arrived a day early and stayed with a nice, fairly well-off family that attended the church. Their home was beautiful. The Sunday service went well and we were voted in.

My family and I then went about looking for housing. Although we didn't find anything, we knew God would provide, and we looked forward to the first Sunday of me being the new pastor.

Everything that first Sunday went great. If I remember correctly, about thirty-five people showed up. God's Spirit was moving. After lunch, Denise and the kids returned to Savannah, Tennessee, to pack our clothes. I decided that the evening service should be a prayer meeting because everyone could use more prayer. I had been to Brownsville Revival Tuesday night prayer meetings and had led those types of meetings at our presbyter's church and other churches. I already had some sheets of paper printed up with words serving as headlines—similar to banners at Brownsville—with the words "Schools," "Government," "Church," "Revival," "Healing," "Families," "Marriages," etc. We were ready to go. Prior to the evening service, I laid the sheets of paper out across the front of the church to use as prayer points.

We began our prayer meeting that night by reading Psalm 139:23-24: "Search me, O God, and know my heart: try me, and know my thoughts: and see if there be any wicked way in me, and lead me in the way everlasting" (KJV). We then spent a few minutes in repentance before praying in tongues according to the exhortation in Jude 1:20 to build ourselves up on our most holy faith, praying in the Holy Spirit. As people's hearts began to be touched, the Holy Spirit began to move. Before long, we had tongues and interpretation. People were weeping. God was moving.

Next, we went through the entire building, praying over it, sweeping the devil out of it. We bound the devil and loosed the Holy Spirit, anointing various spots with oil while believing God to create a holy habitation. We then focused on the small paper banners. Groups of people picked different topics, then joined together and prayed over them. We called to the North, the South, the East, and the West, commanding the gates of the enemy to be broken down, for captives to be set free and to come into the house of the Lord. I thought we were having a great prayer meeting. I would soon find out that not everyone agreed.

Early the next morning, I received a phone call from the superintendent. "Brother Bill," he said, "you're the pastor, you can do what you want. But I've had a few calls today and some people seem to have problems with the prayer meeting. You might want to have a board meeting."

I called the board member that my family and I had been staying with. He wouldn't say much but admitted that others wanted a meeting. So that afternoon, I met with three members of the board. One of them was something of a ring leader. He asked me, "What do you think you're doing? You can't just pray in tongues anytime you want to. You can't tell people to just start praying in tongues. That's charismatic witchcraft." I was stunned. He thought you had to wait until the Spirit hits you or comes on you before you can pray in tongues.

I believe tongues is a gift of God you may use anytime you want. Paul said to "pray with the spirit" and to "pray with the mind also" (see 1 Corinthians 14:15). Everywhere I had been where God was moving and revival was being poured out, there were prayer warriors praying in tongues. I can tell you this: once you start praying in tongues by faith, you will be hit by something—the power of God. In 1 Corinthians 14:2, Paul says that when you speak in a tongue (as when praying in the spirit), you speak to God and not to men. It's a hotline to heaven. Paul goes on to say that he who speaks in a tongue edifies himself and that it's even better to prophesy because prophesying edifies the church (the congregation). So, how can you edify (build up) the church if you yourself aren't edified?

Praying in tongues is like charging your battery so your light will shine on others. Since the day God baptized me in the Spirit, I've had the freedom to pray in tongues at will. The problem with a lot of "Pentecostals" is that they're waiting for a lightning bolt to hit them from heaven, so they only pray or speak in tongues maybe once every five years. There's a difference between a prayer language and a message in tongues with interpretation, initiated by the Holy Ghost as He sees fit. We may exercise our prayer language, in tongues, at will, anytime, anywhere.

I won't go into details of any argument that occurred at the board meeting but will simply say that the other two board members were scared to say much.

It's amazing how some board members want to run their churches. It's the reason some of our churches are in such bad shape. There's no scripture to support board members running the church. The Church is to be overseen by those Jesus gives to be apostles, prophets, evangelists, pastors and teachers. I'm sorry to say that many of those on church boards are not qualified to be deacons or elders. So we call them "board members" and fill the boards with men who have an earthly agenda. A majority of people in our average churches are not very spiritually minded; for if they were, we wouldn't be in the shape that we are today. Many of those on boards wanting to oversee their churches are not qualified to do so. It's a calling, not a voting. I know these are hard words, but it's time for our Bible-believing churches to get back to the Bible. The Church is not a democracy but a theocracy.

Now, on the other hand, the reason we have constitutions and bylaws and boards running churches is because so many pastors have done a poor job when the ball was in their court; misusing finances ... abusing and manipulating the flock ... becoming disreputable throughout town ... not paying bills ... running off with the church secretary. Shame on them.

And shame on us. We have lost the trust and respect of

people around the world. One reason we need true apostles again is to renew the respect and dignity of the calling of God and to call out those leaders who are doing a poor job instead of simply sending them to different locations. It's time for the men and women of God to regain the respect of the world. We need character, dignity, and fearlessness in our pulpits again.

In the area where I live there are about seven thousand people and about fifty churches. It should feel like holy ground when you drive into town. But it doesn't. There is just as much meth, crack, pot, divorce, gangs, suicide, and murder in this place than just about anywhere else in the nation. There must be a problem with the church. We are supposed to bring change, not become accustomed to the world.

Once, I went to Adair County in Kentucky to preach revival. At the time, the county had about seventeen thousand people and two hundred twenty churches. Yet, you would have thought it had only about ten churches as the place was ridden with murder, drugs, alcohol, divorce, and adultery.

We need revival in America. We have churches, but where is the Spirit? Where is the power of God? Our government is not to be blamed. Sinners are not to be blamed. Public schools are not to be blamed. It's the Church's fault. And it begins with the men behind the pulpits. It's time for the Church to rise up and be the voice of America again. I believe that day is coming.

Many of us say we want prophets in the church again. But do we really? Those who could 'read our mail'? What if a prophet walked in and started calling out the sins of the church? That might clear things out in a hurry. Yet, we need the fear of God in our churches again. It's long been missing. There's been no fear of consequence for sin and no spirit of conviction because there's been no Holy Spirit—to speak of—in our churches.

I remember a friend of mine fresh out of Bible school, preaching his first revival. He had asked God for the gifts of the Spirit to flow through him. He wanted prophetic words for the people. You know, 'The blessings are coming. Revelation is coming. God's about to answer and do awesome things in your life.' At the altar call, God revealed to him that the first woman he was about to pray for was in an adulterous relationship. Man, he did not want to give her that word. But eventually he got up the nerve and whispered in her ear, "You're having an affair and you'd better get out of it." She dropped to the floor like a rock, broken and repentant. God restored her marriage. This is the sort of thing we need happening in our churches. I pray, "God, restore the apostles and prophets that the true power of God may bring the fear of the Lord back into our churches."

As I headed home from the board meeting that Monday evening, I called Denise and told her to unpack. I said we weren't going to be moving after all. I was pretty broken-hearted at that point. I didn't know if I ever wanted to try pastoring again. Tears filled my eyes and there was a lump in my throat. Had I missed God that badly? I think so. I think it was me who wanted the church and that it wasn't necessarily the direction God wanted me to go in. It can be easy to try and manipulate God to do what looks good.

Nevertheless, God saved me from a lot of heartache. I would come to find out later that on the night of the vote, the church actually held two votes. The first vote was to determine who should be voted on for the position of pastor: me, or another man who had tried out. I won that one. Then they voted on whether I should actually be their pastor. I won that one too, by a slim margin of 6 to 5. The man my family and I stayed with was the one who had cast the tie-breaker.

So back to Savannah I went. No job. No house. A wife and kids. We did have a small motorhome and travel trailer though. So after a few days of staying with my mother-in-law, Denise and I loaded up the kids and took a trip. What else does an evangelist do when he's down. We went up to Niagara Falls and then into Canada to check out the revival going on in Toronto. That would get me going again.

The fellowship hosting the revival in Toronto was meeting in a large warehouse near the end of a runway of Pearson International Airport. As my family entered the building, we could hear a thunderstorm of prayer going on in a room up above. Most of the fifty or so intercessors in that upper room were praying loudly in tongues. I thought to myself, *I'm in the right place. This brings the power down for revival.* We continued through something of an open bookstore before emerging into a seating area with about five hundred people.

Someone said, "There's a special orchestra from Finland that has been traveling around and tonight they will lead worship." When I heard that, I was kind of bummed. *An orchestra at a revival meeting? What was I in for?* Well, it turned out to be quite a surprise. The orchestra began by warming up their instruments (violins, fiddles, bass fiddles, percussion, etc.) and then just took off in the Spirit, as if all members were playing their own songs, yet all blending together. It was awesome. Later, I found out they had been touched by revival when some of the leaders from Toronto went over to Finland and God touched their orchestra. They were a spirit-filled bunch. I had never heard anything like it. They played for about thirty minutes in the Spirit before the worship team began singing to their music.

After the preaching that night the congregation was told, "Whoever wants prayer, come stand on a red line." So I did. They had red lines running about the altar area to help people from becoming bunched up. My family received prayer. It was just what we needed. People were slain in the spirit, laughing, crying, having visions. God knows what each person needs. We would return the following night for more. The atmosphere was different than what I had experienced at Brownsville, but it was the same Spirit of God moving in our midst.

We spent two great weeks on the road before heading for home. (I was born to travel.) After returning to Savannah, Denise and I were able to purchase a home without any job. (Huh, isn't that interesting.) I worked for a while selling air purifiers, then worked at my next door neighbor's chrome polishing shop. During this time, the family attended First Assembly of God in Savannah under Pastor Gaylon Echols. He was a real blessing and encouragement on our road to recovery.

I was working for my neighbor at $7 an hour when I remembered a man at a yacht dealership having told me that if I ever needed a job, to come see him. Knowing that I had worked on bicycles and motorcycles, he said he could teach me how to work on yachts.

I don't think there was a single Christian among the twenty employees at that dealership. Some gave me a hard time. But that was okay. I was now getting paid $10 an hour and I had a lot of people to witness to. I would also be blessed at the company's 4th of July dinner after getting to the lunchroom a bit late. They kept calling me to hurry and get there, hurry and get there. I thought, *That's funny. They never worried about me getting there before.* When I came through the door, to my surprise I found a big dinner spread out with everybody just standing around, waiting. No one had started eating or doing anything. They said, "Brother Bill, would you please pray over the meal for us?" I about fell out of my shoes. Of course I would bless the meal. It was an exciting moment. And you know, little by little, I gained their respect.

It was while working at the yacht place that God began to put in my heart that I should get a motorcycle and do some racing. I hadn't raced since being saved and was now almost 40 years old. You can get hurt on those things! But it felt like God was clearly telling me to do this and use it as an opportunity to share Jesus with motorcycle racers. It's one thing to simply show up and try to talk to racers; it's another when you suit up and ride with them.

So I went down to Iuka, Mississippi, to talk to a friend of

mine named Benny Weathers about a 1997 Suzuki RMX250 he was trying to sell. He said I could take it out and ride it to see if I liked it. So I dug out some old riding equipment and rode the bike around on some land by my home for a couple of weeks. I got on the Internet and checked out the schedule for the Mid-South Hare Scramble Summer Series. I called the race promoter, told him who I was, and asked if I could say a few words and have prayer before the race. He said to me, "Sometimes another man does that. But if he's not here, you can." Guess what. The other guy didn't show up, but I did.

Now, what do you say to a hundred fifty guys on motorcycles getting ready to race on a Sunday when they should be in church? I'll tell you what. You say to them, "God has a plan for your life. Are you looking for that plan?" You pray for them. You pray for their families. And you pray over the race. You then hop on your bike and take off with them. Perhaps the Church should be going out to such events to try and reach those who are lost. My wife and kids were at that race, handing out Bibles and drinking water.

I had been praying a lot for my own safety in that race because we would be circling around a six- to eight-mile course through woods, over and around all types of obstacles including trees, rocks, and creeks, for upwards of two hours. If you had to stop and get gas, it would add to your time. If you fell down, it would add to your time. First man to cross the finish line inside of two hours was the winner.

Before the race begins, you're sitting on your bike with the engine cut off. There are about twenty different classes organized by engine size, bike frame, and age of riders. Each class lines up in a horizontal row. A man drops his arm, the racers kick start their bikes, and off they go in a wave of motorcycles. A minute later, the next class starts up and takes off. A minute after that, the next class. And so on, until all classes of racers are out on the track at the same time.

My class, the 40-some-year olds, was situated at about Row 18. I was allowed to ride in that class because I had turned 40 that year. As the row ahead of mine took off, I waited and watched … anxious … heart pounding … adrenaline flowing. The man dropped his arm, my bike cranked on the first kick, I gunned it, and hung on for dear life.

Endurance is important in this type of racing. It's not like a sprint where you go a relatively short distance and then you're done. You must keep the bike up and running on two wheels with your body going the entire time.

I finished the scramble within one and a half hours. I almost ran out of body fuel. I was dying. Yet, I managed to finish fourth out of about ten in my class. Despite the physical exhaustion, I believed it was worth the entire effort just to bring a bit of Jesus to a crowd of racers.

It's like that in a life for Christ. It's not about a sprint; it's about the long run. We must run in such a way so as to win the prize of the upward call of God in Christ Jesus. You cannot quit, because if you do, you get a "DNF" (Did Not Finish). We cannot stand before God with a DNF in hand at the end of this race called life.

I raced in seven events that summer with God opening the door for me to speak at each one of them. At one race, I was able to share for about twenty minutes. It was awesome. I used course arrows to talk about the course of life. Other racers started calling me Preacher Man. Once, a young racer came up to me with a jersey full of holes he had cut in it. "Preacher Man," he said, "I wore my holy jersey today." Well, at least I had him thinking.

I think it may have been for the fourth race that I called the promoters to get permission to speak and pray before the start of the race and was told they didn't think there would be time for it. They were trying to put me off. They weren't so sure about having prayer at a race. However, on the day of the race I was at the starting line in a short riders meeting when a truck with two motorcycles arrived late and the promoter said, "We'll take a break while these two guys get unloaded and ready to go. We don't know what we'll do for a couple of minutes, but we'll take a break." I said, "Sir, I'll fill in the break time." He said, "Okay." So I spoke until they got ready. Hoo! God will make a way. It was a rough race that day. I was the only one in my class but did it anyway. Afterwards, as the trophies were being handed out and I went to get mine, the race promoter looked at me and said, "You are welcome to come to any race we have and do what you do." That was great. Jesus was touching their hearts. (Maybe I should become a race chaplain.)

By the end of summer, I had opened each race with prayer. I also prayed at a National Enduro and at a banquet for the Winter Series race. God had opened doors. We need people in every influence of life bringing Jesus to a lost and dying world.

In the last race of the series, I had the points to win my class but took a hard fall on a downhill, cracking at least a couple ribs. I had to get up and finish the lap so I could get back to the motorhome. I was in a lot of pain and passing blood. I had banged up one of my kidneys. It left me in pain for a couple of weeks. It would also be the end of my riding … for a while anyway. I sold the bike as I believed I had accomplished what God had for me to do. It was time to move on.

Even though it had been over a year since I pastored a church, I began feeling an urge to get back into pastoring. I talked to Denise about it. She was in agreement. Having learned about an open position at a church in Northwest Tennessee, I made contact and was invited to come and preach under the stipulation that they were not ready for a pastor yet but would be soon. They were in a new building; a very nice structure with a congregation of about forty people. I preached two services. My messages seemed to be well-received.

By this time, I had changed jobs and was now working for Travis Boating as a service and parts manager with higher pay.

God was providing. I was also working on finishing up three Bible courses to receive ordination papers. In the Assemblies of God, they certify to preach, license to preach, and ordain to preach.

Eventually, I got the call to come try out as the new pastor of the church in Northwest Tennessee. I was excited and ready to get back to pastoring and preaching again—what some would call a "full-time ministry." Truth is, all of us are supposed to be in full-time ministry, regardless of job or occupation.

I went and preached, and the church voted us in … one hundred percent. Praise God. He was on the move again.

5

The Testimony

December 31, 1999. I was standing on the platform at the Brownsville Revival. We were there to bring in the New Year on the eve of "the new millennium" or, "Y2K." For most of the year, Americans had been warned to stay home on this night because no one knew how computers would handle the change from 1999 to 2000. Many predicted banks would fail, businesses would shut down, and gas stations would close as power plants failed. I thought, *What better place to be than revival.* Some had even said Jesus would be coming back then. I figured we couldn't lose being at revival. I didn't have a clue what was really about to happen.

A newspaper had reported that guest evangelist Steve Hill would be preaching the message of a lifetime that night. Who was to know he wouldn't. I was standing on the platform after being chosen to share a short testimony of something that had happened to me at the revival. That should have been easy enough to do. I had been coming as often as I could since April 1996, leading three bus trips and several van trips, as well as making perhaps over twenty trips by myself. I was hungry to be with God. And every trip was an adventure.

My first bus trip down was with a group of men from Milan, Tennessee. Their pastor, Bill Lickliter, had invited another pastor friend and me to go along with them. Milan First Assembly had been holding revival meetings on Friday nights. My friend and I went up there as often as we could. The women and youth of that church were on fire for God, but it hadn't really hit the men yet. It was going to be one memorable trip to Brownsville.

We drove most of Wednesday night to reach Pensacola by morning and get in line outside the church in time to secure seats in the main sanctuary. The men joked and played cards all the way down. They didn't have a clue that God was about to radically change their lives. One touch from His hand and you're never the same. God had a plan for those guys. I think He set them up. Checking into our motel on Thursday, I got a room by myself several rooms down from everybody else.

That night, Brother Steve Hill preached about 'holding the cards.' "You are willing to give up certain things," he said, "but you don't want to give it all up. You want to hold onto some of those cards." Holding up extra large cards in his hand, he said, "You will give up alcohol or drugs, but you don't want to give up pornography and lust."

Now, one of the men in our group had a deck of cards in his pocket. During the altar call, Steve Hill looked right at the area where the men were sitting and said, "One of you is still holding the cards, and I would come point you out, but God is waiting on you to give them up." Of course, it wasn't the cards Brother Steve was talking about, but sin. Several of the guys were holding onto the pew in front of them with a death grip. Suddenly, one of them busted loose and ran to the altar. I think all them wound up making things right with God over the next two days. One of them was even a Ku Klux Klan member who gave his life to Jesus and would see his marriage and entire life restored.

But it was after returning to our motel the second night that things got crazy. Just about the time I was falling asleep, around 2:30 AM, I received a phone call. It was one of the guys that had ridden down in the back of the bus. He said, "We have this Baptist doctor down here who wants to be baptized in the Holy Ghost. Would you come down and help us pray for him?" I said, "Yes." I put on some clothes and headed down to their room.

When I arrived, I found that a few of the men who had been playing cards on the bus ride down were there. The doctor was sitting on a bed. An older minister there said to me, "I've been telling him about the Holy Ghost." The doctor said, "All I know is I want everything God has for me." I told him to raise his hands. When he did, I slapped them and said, "More, Lord!" The power of God hit him like a strong electrical current. He shot back on the bed and began speaking in tongues.

About that time, Heaven invaded the room. One of the men began to go into deep intercession with loud groaning, sounding as though he'd been hit in the stomach with a fist. Another began to weep and cry and would end up going through almost an entire box of tissues. A guy standing by the door began to shake—especially his arms. Then the doctor hit the floor, face down on his knees, and began pushing himself about the floor. By the time he got up, he had carpet burns on his forehead.

God's power hit that room like a bomb going off. Lives were being changed. Two other guys hearing the noise from a nearby room came over and were immediately hit by the power of God. All of us were under the influence of the Holy Spirit when, at about 4:30 AM, one of the guys said, "Call our wives and tell them to stop praying! They're about to kill us!" Their wives had set aside that Friday night after the Milan Revival service to fast and pray for their husbands to have an encounter with God like they had experienced. It was awesome.

God's presence was in that room like it had been on the day of Pentecost. My senses could feel the glory of God. It was weighty or, heavy and it affected everyone in a different way. It was as if God had put a warm, energized wet blanket on us, but without getting any of us wet. And although each man experienced something different, the outcomes were similar: lives changed for the better with deliverance and healing. No longer would they be men ashamed of serving Jesus, but men who would arrive to church early and leave late; men who would go up to the front of the church openly worshipping God, their marriages restored. It's amazing what the presence of God can do for a person in such a short time. He is our Creator and Designer. He knows how to fix us and will *if* we allow Him to.

Eventually, things began to settle down in the motel room as the glory lifted and we were able to get in a few hours sleep before riding the bus back to Milan.

We were loaded in the bus, ready to go, when Pastor Bill got up and said, "We're going to sing a song and then we're going to have some testimonies." We didn't get through that song before the presence of God manifested right there on the bus and remained with us the entire way back! (The trip was documented in a video entitled, *The Miracle of Pensacola*.)

On another trip down to Pensacola, I took with me Pastor David, an evangelist. Our plan was to spend three days at Brownsville just prior to his preaching revival at my church in Bolivar. I wanted him to experience what I had. Following the service on the third night, we returned to my van in the parking lot where I asked him, "What do you think about it? The revival." He said, "I don't know. It was good singing and preaching, but it was so crowded. I really didn't have room to get loosened up." About that time, the Spirit of God hit him right there in the front captain's seat of my Ford Aerostar. He began rocking back and forth. I thought he was going to tear the seat from the floor. Suddenly, he popped the door open and took off running in circles around the parking lot like Speedy Gonzales, throwing gravel everywhere.

You just never know where or how God is going to hit you. And I'm telling you, revival in Bolivar that next week was awesome. David preached like a man on fire. People were saved. About twenty-three were baptized in water. People were baptized in the Holy Ghost. And there were healings.

God has a purpose for what He does. I think when Pastor David took off running outside the Brownsville church that third night, God broke some religious things off of him, because he was now preaching with great freedom.

I could tell you story after story of people being affected in the Brownsville Revival. I loved to take car-loads, van-loads, and bus-loads of people to that revival because I knew their lives would be changed, that God would touch them and meet their needs. I never had a trip where God didn't do something awesome. No two trips were the same.

Fast-forward to the end of 1999. I was now pastoring a church in Sidonia, Tennessee. I'd been there since October. A number of people in the church were hungry for more of God, most of them new members. We had been having weeknight home meetings in which I would show Brownsville videos and then pray for people. In those meetings the presence of God would come just as He had in the motel room with the men from Milan. At some point, those in attendance would find it impossible to stand up. With God's weighty presence in the house, people would be laid out all over the floor. They would shake, cry, be healed, set free, delivered. It wasn't long before they began inviting other people to come to the meetings. It was great.

Some of them began to say, "We want to go down there [to Brownsville] and visit the revival." So I began praying about it and decided New Year's weekend would be a great time to attend. About fourteen people decided to go.

We took two vans. All the way down I was telling people, "You just don't know what is going to happen to you in the next couple of nights. You just don't know." Fact is, I didn't have anymore of a clue than they did as to what God was going to pull off that New Year's Eve.

We made it to Brownsville, got checked into our motel rooms, and headed to church. The waiting line outside wasn't bad at this point in the revival and so we were able to get into the main sanctuary with good seats in the middle toward the front.

Worship was great as usual. Then Dr. Michael Brown came out and said they were going to have some testimonies. He gave a thirty-minute explanation on how to give a five-minute testimony. John Kilpatrick, pastor of the church, then got up and said, "We'll have one more worship song and then, if you have a testimony about something that happened to you at Brownsville, stay standing when the worship music stops." I began to think, *I have a lot of testimonies. Maybe I should stay standing.* But I was not sure. *Which one would I give?* I asked myself. *If he picks me to testify, then it's God's will.*

The music stopped. I remained standing. Pastor Kilpatrick began to choose those who would testify. If I remember correctly, he picked about six people, then said, "One more," and picked me.

My legs began to weaken as I walked up onto the platform. Electricity was in the air. When I say "electricity," I mean the anointing of God. The power and presence of God were in the air. Two women testified ahead of me. As it got closer to my turn, my knees became weaker, my heart beat rapidly, and my mind was racing. I asked God, *What am I gonna say? What am I gonna say?* In reply, it was as if He said to me, "Shut up, stupid. I'm fixin' to tell you what to say." Then came my turn.

I started out kind of slow. But a storm was brewing inside of me. I got to feeling that if I didn't let some words out, I would blow up. The Holy Ghost began to possess me and take over. It felt as though power flowed out of my body with each word that I spoke. My mind was trying to comprehend what was going on as my spirit man took over. I talked beyond my allotted five minutes, but Pastor Kilpatrick kept holding the microphone up to my mouth, going with the flow. People were standing up, shouting, clapping. It was on!

After a while, Pastor Kilpatrick directed the ushers to have those who were waiting to testify after me to return to their seats. He continued holding the mic to my face. He even called for my group to come up onto the stage. Eventually, he handed me the mic, saying, "Here, I'm tired of holding this." I would end up speaking for over 40 minutes! At the end, Pastor Kilpatrick called on Steve Hill to come and pray over me and the group. As Steve laid on hands, each and every one of us went down under the power of God.

Brother Steve did not preach that night. Instead, some hillbilly from Tennessee preached the millennium service of the longest running revival in the history of America. What were the chances of that happening? You know, if God had asked me, "What would you like to do?" I would have said, "Preach at Brownsville." Now, in the natural realm there was no way that was going to happen. I was a nobody; just a pastor of a small church in Tennessee. Yet, like Psalm 37:4 says, "Delight yourself in the Lord; and He will give you the desires of your heart." You see, preaching at Brownsville is something I did not have the faith to pray or ask for. I had been greatly satisfied in simply taking others to the revival. But God's plan for me was greater than my own.

They had to sort of carry me off the platform that night. A man seated in the front got up and they put me in his place. I sat there for a minute, but then slipped right out and onto the floor like a dead man. The heavy presence, that weighty glory of God, was so strong that I could not remain seated in the chair, let alone stand up. The anointing was on me and increasing beyond anything I had ever experienced before. It wasn't so much for changing my life, but for equipping me for future ministry. I could do nothing for the remainder of the service but simply lie flat on the floor.

Announcements were made, someone welcomed in the new year, and they began shutting things down. "We will see you tomorrow night," someone said. There wasn't any additional prayer. The only other person I know of who had been touched as powerfully as I had been was the guy who had given me his seat. After I fell out, he went ahead and sat back down, only to experience the power of God in such a way that he too slid right out of the chair. Before I could get up from the floor, a lady came by, put a hundred-dollar bill in my hand, and spoke over me some words I don't remember.

I had an encounter that evening. It was part of my journey. And my life would never be the same. God had lit a fire in me that would not go out. He was taking me to a higher level.

God can and will do the same for you if you let Him. Moving to the next level is never an easy path. But consider this: Why would God choose some hillbilly pastor out of nowhere to give a message at Brownsville for a coming millennium? Maybe it's because He sees and knows, even if no one else does. When you're serving God with your whole heart, good things happen.

Maybe you're already preaching on street corners, feeding the hungry, clothing the naked, quietly going about your journey, trying to serve God, yet feeling like you're alone and that no one cares. I'm here to tell you that God cares and He sees everything you're doing. If you remain faithful, He will show up suddenly when you least expect it and will so fill you up that it will run out onto others.

I believe every great man or woman of God has a special encounter with God somewhere along the way. Abraham did. Moses did. Daniel did. Peter did. James did. John did. Paul did. God will meet with you as well ... if you go after Him.

I was so blessed by the encounter and opportunity at Brownsville that New Year's Eve night. Even if I wasn't to see any results from it, it would have been totally satisfying.

The Bible tells the story about a blameless, upright man named Job who went through a period of time where God tested and tried him. In the end, he said to the Lord, "I have heard of You by the hearing of the ear; but now my eye sees You" (Job 42:5). God will take you through encounters so that you may go from hearing about Him to seeing Him ... and knowing Him.

Knowing God brings great faith. The Bible says that faith comes by hearing, and hearing by the word of God. That word "word" is translated from the Greek word pronounced *hray'-mah* (transliterated *rhema*). It means "utterance," as by a voice, of something specific. It may imply a fresh word from heaven, because when you hear *rhema* from above, great faith comes to you as you hear and understand what it is that God is saying to you. When you have not simply read the Word of God but have heard God's voice, it brings great faith by which you can accomplish great things. An encounter with God can lead you into a place of being able to hear His voice. In His presence, He desires to speak to you.

To share testimony at a historic revival was exceedingly and abundantly above and beyond anything I could have believed or asked for. It's like Daddy giving his kid a trip to Disneyland but more, so much more. I was blessed just to be a blessing. Our purpose in life is to be used by God to fulfill our destiny and to help others fulfill theirs. My experience at Brownsville that New Year's Eve was just part of my journey into the apostolic.

Interestingly, a few years prior, I had actually laid aside the word spoken to me about being called to be an apostle as I had no comprehension as to what it meant to be one. But God had not forgotten, and the encounter at Brownsville was part of that journey; yet another step down the road that God was having me walk on. Often, God demonstrates before He teaches. What I had seen and experienced at Brownsville would be explained to me later by Him.

Our church group spent two nights in Pensacola. On the

second night, as we were leaving the church, a man came up to me and handed me a gallon can of olive oil. I had never been given a gift like that before. Strangely, the man didn't seem too happy about giving it to me. And before I could ask him about it, he had turned and left. On the side of the can were his name and address. His name was John and he lived in Brownsville—right across the street from the church, in fact. His telephone number was also on the can.

After returning home and pulling myself together some, I called John to find out more about the can of oil. He told me that his daughter had given him the oil for Christmas. It was for anointing.

I'm thinking, *What kind of man has a daughter who gives him a one-gallon can of anointing oil for Christmas?*

John said he had taken the can of oil to Brownsville's school of ministry and had the professors, leaders, and students pray over it, after which he placed it in the church sanctuary, on a prayer table that held pictures of loved ones being prayed for in regard to healing, deliverance, and salvation. The church pastors and intercessors had prayed over the can as it sat on the table. John was then going to pour the oil into small bottles and hand them out to people as God may instruct him.

"But," he said, "God told me to give you the whole can, and I didn't want to do it. Then, as I was walking across the parking lot, he told me again to give it to you. I really didn't want to, but I had to obey God; so I came back to the church and gave it to you even though I wasn't happy about it."

Wow. Hearing that, I knew there had to be something special about this oil. I presumed God had a plan for it. And He did. For John also said that the Lord told him to tell me to take it back and spread it out over Tennessee.

And I intended to do just that ... by His word. Amen.

6

The Can Of Oil

Brownsville had become a launch pad from which the direction of my life changed. Never again would I be satisfied with status quo church, no matter what the cost. The sort of things that had been going on at Brownsville were now breaking out in my church in Sidonia. As I anointed people with the oil from the can that John had given me, they would be hit with the power of God.

One teenage girl was hit by the power, fell to the church floor, and lay there praying in tongues. She then preached, prophesied, and shook. This went on for over two hours. When church was over, someone called her father, requesting that he come and get her because God was touching her so powerfully. The man was afraid to come because he had been away from God. So he sent his wife. When the mother arrived and saw her girl on the floor, shaking and prophesying, unable to get up, she said, "What's wrong with my daughter?" I said to her, "I am not sure, but I think God is touching her." We picked her up and carried her out.

While such things may seem strange to the natural mind, I'm telling you that girl had a life-changing encounter that night and it wasn't long before she started a Bible club at her junior high school.

On another night, a young man became slain in the Spirit and could not get up. We had to put him in a wheelchair, roll him out to his family's van, and drive him across the street where we carried him into his house.

When teenagers are touched by the power of God, something really happens. The sad part about what I was witnessing is that a lot of the adults were on the side watching instead of getting in and going after God.

There was an impartation in the oil from that can. We began pouring it into small bottles and handing those out. Some kids would anoint their schools with the oil. Some would anoint the sick with it. Some prayed over their homes with it. As word about the oil got around, I felt a need to make a trip down to the Savannah area to visit my friend Monty.

Monty ran a tire store in Crump. Dropping in at his store, I told him about my encounter at Brownsville ... and the oil. He took me into his office which was in a house in front of the store. I opened the can, poured out some of the oil, anointed Monty, and the power hit. We went into strong travailing and weeping. It felt like we were giving birth. I wondered, *What is this?* I had seen it happen to ladies, but not to men. Our uncontrollable intercession lasted upwards of forty-five minutes, leaving a pool of tears on the floor. It was very emotional and physical—groaning and travailing that could not be understood. Something had broken into the Spirit realm. It was Romans 8:26 in action: "...the Spirit Himself intercedes for us with groanings too deep for words." The experience left me physically drained.

Since I was in the area, I thought I might as well visit the local Christian television station to see if they would be interested in watching a Brownsville video and allow me to pray over them. They were off the air when I showed up. They put on the video and, as they began to watch it, the power of God filled the studio. I told them about the one-gallon can of oil and the anointing that was with it. They said, "Get it out and anoint the station, and let's pray." So I got it out and began to anoint and pray. First, I prayed over the electronics area. Then I prayed over the sound room and the stage. I prayed and prophesied over the entire place; not me, but the Spirit on me. And just like at Monty's store, the groaning, travailing, prophesying, and weeping began. Next thing I knew, I was down on the floor in a puddle of tears. Man, God exploded in that place.

The station invited me to come back a few weeks later for their share-a-thon fundraiser, which I did, and again the power of God lit up the place. People who were going to sing or participate in the event in some way or another were in the audience watching. As I ministered on television, God began to move on them.

A grandfather led his grandson to the Lord after the Holy Spirit brought conviction upon the boy and he sat in his chair shaking. The grandson then got up, came on stage, and began praying for people. God's presence was touching the audience. I was witnessing the same thing that would repeatedly happen at Brownsville: get saved, get touched, give it away.

A woman dying of liver cancer made her way in after watching the program at home. Doctors had told her she had only a few days to live. The Lord told her to get down to the station. She got up from her sick bed and family members brought her in. We prayed for her right there on the set and God healed her. She would look just fine the next time I saw her a few years later.

At one point, a man burst through the stage doors, running and falling to the platform on his face, repenting. When he was able to talk, he told us that while watching the program at home, great conviction had come upon him, and so he got in his car and started driving to the station, not even knowing where it was. He was a backslidden youth pastor. God led him right to the station some 28 miles from his home and totally restored him.

Many more miracles happened that night that I believe were due to the prayer and intercession over the oil at Brownsville. God was beginning to open doors.

The local newspaper in Martin, Tennessee, sent out a female reporter to interview me concerning the testimony I had given at Brownsville. I gave her a copy of it. She watched it, then interviewed me, and wrote up a great article for the paper.

After sending videos of the testimony to various Christian television stations, I got a call from Nashville where the old Twitty City had been, now home to the TBN Nashville station. They asked me to come and do an interview and show the video. I got up early and made the three-hour drive to Nashville, taking my can of oil with me. The studio I visited was on the TBN campus but associated with a different Christian cable network covering the Nashville area.

The network had arranged for me to be interviewed by a pastor in a one-hour, on-stage segment concerning the video and the oil. The two of us conversed a while, the station ran the video, and then we wrapped up the interview. There was no studio audience; just the camera men, some others, the pastor, and his wife. They asked me to pray with the oil. So I opened the top and poured some out. It was on again! The power of God hit that place like a bomb. I began to prophesy and pray for them. When I anointed them with the oil, they hit the floor.

The station subsequently asked me to do an on-air teaching segment, which I did, but only for a while as it was too far for me to drive to do anything on a regular basis. I nonetheless received phone calls from people who said they had seen the station's airing of the Brownsville testimony and that it really touched their lives.

Things were good and I was excited by all that was

happening. I thought God was going to put me on a platform and launch me out to preach revivals all over ... that I had arrived. But He had other plans for me as another storm was brewing. This one from the devil.

It was time for the yearly business meeting at the church in Sidonia. I wasn't good with these sort of meetings. For one thing, I wasn't allowed to see the church budget until the night of the meeting even though I was the pastor and the one conducting the meeting.

On the agenda was the election of board members. The only qualification for getting on the board of this church was to be a member for one year and receive a majority vote. Sounded like a community club to me.

Now, I don't want to sound harsh, but somebody needs to address these sort of issues in our churches. We overlook them year after year and then wonder why our churches don't grow. It's because they are not in God's order or His plan for a New Testament church.

Well, the minutes were read and the finances — scribbled on notebook paper — were reviewed. I had previously asked several times to see the church books but was never allowed to even though in the end the pastor has a responsibility with regard to the finances of the church and will one day have to stand before God and give account of things. The pastor doesn't have to sign all the checks, but he at least needs to see what's coming in and going out and be allowed to provide some input. From the church body's point of view, too many pastors had come in and wrecked the church's finances, not paid bills, and then left town, leaving the church indebted and with a bad name throughout town. Shame on them ... and us!

Next item on the agenda: nomination of board members. In attendance was a man who, along with his family, hadn't been to church for about three months because, well, he really didn't like me. He showed up for this meeting though. Another man in attendance was a licensed minister who also happened to be a member of the church, which shouldn't have been allowed as it was against protocol in that it presented a potential conflict of interest. Only the night before I had dinner with him at his home as my wife and kids were out of town.

I won't mention any names because the only point in my telling this story is to simply give you an example of some of the crazy things that go on in many of our churches, leaving us with a question as to how we can expect a move of God with this kind of stuff going on.

The licensed minister, who shouldn't have been acting as a voting member, nominated the man who hadn't been in church for three months. What's up with that? I'll tell you what. It was a strategy of the devil for the man who didn't like anything about me to get on the church board. There was no logical reason for the nomination. I thought to myself, *This is not right.* But what was I to do. I'll tell you what. I opened my Bible to 1 Timothy 3:8-13 and read the qualifications of a deacon. I believed God had given me a plan.

I made a motion to retain the current board members for another year while I taught on the qualifications a board member should have and the responsibilities that go with the position. It would be a simple YES-NO vote. A vote of NO meant we would continue with the process of nominating and voting for board members. The church had about twenty-five voting members. The majority voted YES.

After the meeting, the man who couldn't get on the board went into a rage. He went around to board members, blasting them verbally, telling them how unqualified they were and how qualified he was. He called out any faults he saw in them. It was embarrassing. He then came to me and told me how I had embarrassed him in front of everyone by implying that he was not qualified. He told me that God hated me and that one day I would come to his home crawling on my hands and knees, asking for his forgiveness. I didn't say a word; I just let him blow.

After he left, I called the board together and told them there needed to be some discipline for the man. I said he should not be allowed to come into God's house and act the way he did. They said, "Don't worry. It will be okay. He will get over it." I said his membership should be suspended until he repents to the church and shows over a period of time that he can behave himself. The board decided against it, overruling me; and so nothing was done about it.

This is not scriptural! When church leaders allow such a man to continue in wicked ways, wreaking havoc in the church, he becomes a problem for any preacher in that church. Sorry, friends, but some people need to be corrected. For a man on the path of life will heed instruction, but the one who ignores correction goes astray (see Proverbs 10:17). I came to understand why this church had board members instead of deacons. Had there been spiritual leadership in the church, the sort of ridiculous stuff I was having to deal with wouldn't have been allowed to continue because the leadership would have known that one day they will have to stand before God and give account.

Sadly, there wasn't much interest in revival among the leadership either. The board members had the attitude of, "Pastor, we will be there Sunday and Wednesday, but we're not coming any other days. Why don't you just preach and visit the elderly and everything will be all right." *All right? You must be crazy,* I thought. *God has commanded us to go and make disciples of all nations.* I quickly came to realize that I had a choice to make: I could stay at this church another ten years and try to build a team of spiritual leaders that had the same passion I did, or leave and ask God to send me to a place where people were hungry for Him.

The wind had been taken out of my sail. I asked God, "You have been moving in a mighty way, and people have been getting saved, healed, and delivered. Now I face this." There was a holy indignation building up inside of me. As a minister, you have to love people and hate the devil. When God is moving, attacks will come. Unfortunately, many people give up and turn back when those attacks come.

I had a choice to make: stay, or go. I was willing to do either but needed to find out what God wanted me to do. I did not want to put down the can of oil (representing the anointing) to make things easy. For wherever I opened that can and anointed people with the oil, supernatural things would happen. But having that much oil can be a point of contention spiritually.

Many people are satisfied with just enough oil to get them through the week, if but a couple drops. Imagine me putting a couple drops of oil on your head to last you a week. Maybe even three drops. It might be enough to get you through the week, but nobody around you notices that little bit of anointing you have and so, it doesn't cause much conflict. It makes for an easier life to have a minimal anointing or even no anointing. But that's not what God intended. He wants us anointed to invade the gates of hell and you cannot do that with a three-drop anointing. Spiritually-speaking, you need the whole can poured out on you!

If I poured an entire gallon of oil on you, you would be soaked from head to toe. When you left church, the door would be anointed anywhere you touched it. Your car would be anointed where you touched the door handle, where you got in, where you sat in the seat. Everything next to you, even near you, would be affected by that oil. That's the way it's supposed to be spiritually.

There should be enough oil or, anointing in your life to affect the environment around you. If you went into a convenience store, there should be oil on the doors, on the floor, on your purchases, on the counter … even on the workers! It should be at your home and at your job. Oil should be everywhere!

Granted, being that heavily anointed might cause some people to look at you funny. And some people won't like it. It might become uncomfortable for some to sit in your oily seat. It may cause discomfort, even conflict, but it is the only thing that will bring change in our churches, our nation, and our world. Without the anointing, we can do nothing of spiritual significance.

That gallon can of oil was having a big impact on my life. I refused to put it in a closet and try to be a Christian without the anointing, regardless of the cost.

7

The Bike Ride

It was a time of decision. What was I going to do? What did the future hold? What did God want from me?

The secret to making it through trials and tribulations is to find out the will of God for your life. And there's only one way to do that: by praying and seeking God's face until you hear from heaven. So I set myself to pray. Because my family and I lived within only a hundred yards of the church, every day I would go there at about eleven o'clock in the morning and stay until about one or two in the afternoon praying ... seeking the Lord ... worshiping Him.

A lady in the church had made some flags or, banners. I waved those banners, praising God and crying out to heaven, saying, "God, I need an answer because I want to be obedient. I don't want to miss You. And I don't want to set the can of oil down. I refuse to go on with life in an easy, satisfied manner. God, I want to see the anointing. I want to see revival. I want to see an outpouring of your Holy Spirit. Send me, or use me here, whatever You want to do, but I want to be around people that are hungry for You, and I want to see the fire of God burning." I visited the church daily for about three weeks. The anointing was there. His presence was there. But I didn't hear anything from Him.

The church had been holding weekly intercessory prayer meetings and people were coming. And God was still leading me to go out and pray for people. Oil from the gallon can had been poured into little bottles and distributed, and people were taking it all about the region. On one occasion, I spoke at the First Assembly of God Church in Milan concerning the ministry of the Brownsville video and the can of oil. People came to the altars to receive prayer. Some came dumping out pill bottles. We poured oil into those pill bottles. We poured oil into various types of containers that people took with them. The oil and the anointing were still flowing. But I needed to hear from heaven.

After three weeks of daily prayer and worship time at the church, I returned to the parsonage one afternoon to find no one home as Denise had left with the kids for a while. So I decided to take a bath. I drew my water, got in, and was just lying there in the tub, taking a nice bath ... relaxing ... minding my own business ... when all of a sudden the Word of the Lord came and God spoke to me saying, "This is what I want you to do: I want you to ride a bicycle across America. I want you to pray over state capitols. I want you to pray 2 Chronicles 7:14—"[If] My people who are called by My name humble themselves and pray and seek My face and turn from their wicked ways, then I will hear from heaven, will forgive their sin and will heal their land." He concluded, "This is what I want you to do. Believe Me for revival in America."

I was pretty stunned. I had been expecting God. But not like that! So I had a question for Him: "Lord, I've been at the church praying three weeks now, about two to three hours every day, worshiping and seeking Your face. Why are you speaking to me here in the bath tub?" Here's what I heard from the Lord: "You're doing all the talking while you're at the church. But when you were here in the bath tub, you were quiet and I was able to talk to you."

You know, a lot of times when we're praying we think we have to be active and we've got to be speaking words and crying out to God. But I'm here to tell you there are times when we just need "Peace. Be still." We need to be quiet before the Lord and listen for His voice so we can hear Him when He speaks to us.

I got to wondering, *What am I going to do now? How am I going to do this? How does one pray over a state capitol?* I had ridden bicycle before, so I didn't consider that to be a really great challenge. But it had been about ten years and I wasn't in very good shape at this time. Yet, God had so touched my heart.

If you're going to do something for God, you need to hear from Him. The Bible says that faith comes by hearing, and hearing by the word of God. You need *rhema* — that word from heaven — if you are going to fulfill a task that God has assigned to you.

In May of 2000 I began to make arrangements for the ride. I planned to resign from the church on Mother's Day, which was about two weeks out. I talked to the presbyter and he said, "Okay, if that's what God's told you to do, you need to do it." Later, he received a call from the district superintendent who said to him, "You need to talk to Bill. He's gone crazy. What is the deal over there?" In response, the presbyter said, "I'm just glad that God didn't tell me to do that, so I'm not going to tell him anything."

A lot of other people thought, *What do you think you're doing? You're leaving a church. You're getting paid a salary. You have a house to live in and need to take care of your children. And you're just going to go on the road, ride a bicycle, and start praying?*

Ever since my early years in ministry, I had wanted to see God move. I wanted to be like the men of old that I had read about; men like Smith Wigglesworth and John G. Lake who just traveled down the road, encountered God, and had their needs met by Him. Sometimes we trust too much in what we can do. We trust in our jobs. We trust in our finances. We trust in our insurance. We trust in all the wrong things. I wanted to see God move.

I'll tell you, when God opens the door for you to do something, it won't necessarily be easy. Faith is risky. You don't know what's out in the deep water. You don't know what the next day may hold. Yet, it's exciting to live a life of faith. So on Mother's Day I went ahead and resigned from my position as pastor of the church.

I had a little motorhome all ready to go: a 24-foot Class C rig. I contacted a friend of mine from West Virginia named Wayne who I had met at a Whataburger in Pensacola the night of my New Year's Eve testimony. He and his wife had moved to Florida to attend the Brownsville Revival School of Ministry. I asked him if he would be interested in driving the motorhome a couple weeks in support of my ride. He was up for that. I had planned to begin the ride on June 1, accompanied by my son and another young man from church named Greg who believed God was speaking to his heart about it.

After resigning from the church in Sidonia, Denise and I took our kids and motorhome to a place we had purchased in Adamsville, Tennessee. I got to thinking, *God, you really didn't give me direction. Where do I start at this? What state capitol? How do I do it? I haven't read any books on how to do it.* It soon came to me that if we were going to carry revival across the U.S., we should start at Brownsville, in Pensacola, where God had been pouring out His Spirit. So Denise and I drove our motorhome and another vehicle down to Florida. Accompanying us was Greg along with his wife and mother in their car. Wayne provided lodging for both of our families.

I came to believe that the first capital God wanted us to ride to was Montgomery, Alabama. Greg, my son, and I did a few rides around town to get in better shape before we set out on our journey. One day, we cycled over the Pensacola Bay Bridge. Just to the east of that bridge and closer to the water was an older bridge serving as a fishing pier. Riding out onto that pier, I noticed three crosses affixed to the railing facing the larger bridge. The crosses were spaced a good distance one from another. There I found John, the same John who only five months prior had given me the gallon can of oil. I had been told I would likely find him on the pier. In summertime, he and others undertook a forty-day fast, tying three crosses to the bridge railing and spending time on the pier, day and night, praying and seeking the Lord. The crosses served as a witness to those crossing the bay northward from Gulf Breeze via the newer, higher bridge.

In fellowshipping with John, he said to me, "Bill, why don't you stand here and put your hands on the cross." Talk about a life-changing experience. I took a stand on the curb and, facing the cross, put my hands up on it about where Jesus might have had His when He was crucified. Just a glimpse into what the Lord experienced on the cross. The cross stood about six feet in height. With the sun up behind me, I looked down at the ocean water and saw the shadow of the cross with my body on it. I could almost see in the eyes of those who looked at the cross while passing by on the higher bridge. Though they looked right at me, it was as if the cross was a shield in front of me. I imagine many of them wondered, *What are you doing? That's crazy.* I believed conviction was coming with a reminder of what took place on Calvary nearly two thousand years ago. It gave me power. It was a revelation of the power of the cross that goes before us. It was awesome. I could not feel the stares of the people; only the glory of the cross shining in their eyes.

After holding onto the cross a while, my arms got tired. It made me think about Jesus hanging on the cross and how his arms must have become extremely fatigued. Yet, He stayed the course. I knew that I too would have to stay the course.

After coming down from the cross, I talked with John

about it and told him my companions and I were going to be praying over state capitols. Pointing to a cross on the railing some yards away, he said, "Brother Bill, I have a cross down there … the third one. Why don't you take it with you?" And so we did.

Soon, it came time for us to begin our ride to Montgomery. On the first day, early in the week, we pedaled our lightweight road bikes a good distance before calling it a day and returning in the motorhome to rest with our families. The following morning, Denise and Greg's wife returned to Tennessee in the cars we had driven down. Wayne returned us cyclists to the spot where we had stopped the day before and from there we continued our ride.

It was hot that week in southern Alabama. Really hot. I don't know if it was caffeine withdrawals, the devil, the heat, or what, but I ended up with an intense, splitting headache. I eventually had to send the other two cyclists on up ahead of me. Wayne also went ahead to find a place for us to stay that night. At one point, I stopped in at a little store and laid my head on a table there, thinking I was going to get sick. After awhile, the storekeeper said, "I'm fixin' to close and you've got to go." He offered no help. I continued on, stopping at some houses along the way, knocking on doors in hopes of obtaining some relief. But none would come. I managed to get fairly close to Troy when Wayne returned in the motorhome. I took a few aspirins and rested in the cool awhile before we finally made it to town.

I had previously given some friends from Troy a copy of the Brownsville testimony. After watching it, they said, "Please come to our church." At the time, I said to them, "Give this tape to your pastor and let him watch it and see if he's interested." When I got in touch with them later, they said he was interested. We would end up spending the night at their church. It was a Vineyard church.

I had never really been to a Vineyard church before, but I knew they believed in the working of the Holy Spirit. We were allowed to do the service that evening and had a great time. The worship was great. I preached and prayed for people.

At the end of the service, the pastor came to me and said, "The elders would like to see you and your team in the back room." I thought, *Oh no. Maybe we did something wrong. I'm not sure what they believe or of their doctrine exactly, but maybe something was out of alignment here.* Fear came into my heart.

We went into the back room. The pastor said, "Many years ago when I started my ministry here in Alabama, I was in Birmingham, and I preached at a church where they called me to the back, and the pastor and his elders brought out some water and washed my feet and prayed over me, and said, 'We believe that you're in the will of God and we confirm what you're doing and we want to bless you.'" He continued, "We want to do that for you and your team tonight. Our elders and I want to wash your feet, pray over you, bless you, and confirm that we believe you have heard from God and you want to do God's work."

That was exciting and a great relief. Actually, it was awesome because for the past few weeks I believed the enemy had come against me, saying, "What do you think you're doing? You've left security. Here you are. You don't know how you can feed your family. They paid your house notes, but now you have no promise of anything, and you're out here riding a bicycle around, praying and believing God for revival." So, to have this church standing behind us, praying for us, was a confirmation.

God will confirm whatever He sends you out to do. As you move out to fulfill *rhema*, the word that God has spoken to you, God will confirm it through the voices of others.

The following morning, we determined that we were fairly close to Montgomery … within about fifty miles. So we decided to drive to the capitol to find out what it takes to pray over it. I didn't know what we were supposed to do. We drove into the city, found a parking spot fairly close to the capitol, walked around to the front, and went inside.

Looking around, we found a man sitting at a desk. I asked

him if we could pray inside the capitol. He said he didn't know, that he'd have to find out from someone else ... who had to ask someone else ... who had to ask someone else. Eventually, it came back down the line and he said, "You cannot pray in the state capitol, but you can pray out on the front steps. You can set a time tomorrow." We arranged for 12:00–1:00 PM the following day. The man said, "You can have the front steps. You can bring your people, and you can bring a sound system and speakers, or whatever you want to do. You can have a prayer meeting here on the front steps." I said, "Well, I don't have a sound system and I don't have any people ... just us four here ... but we will come and pray." We were given a state capitol parking permit that would allow us to park directly across from the front of the capitol building the following day.

We returned to Troy and had a good night's sleep. Arising early the next morning, we saddled up and headed for Montgomery. We made it to town around 10:30 or 11:00 AM and rode our bikes all the way to the capitol. Wayne was there waiting with the motorhome parked in the right spot. It had been a great ride. We stood before the capitol steps and prayed a bit, but since it wasn't noon yet, we went and put our bikes back behind the motorhome.

Tied to the back of the RV was the cross John had given us to take on our journey. I told the others, "We're going to untie the cross when it's our time, we're going to go up on those steps, and we're going to pray. We then sat down inside the motorhome to have some lunch. Wayne was fasting for us, as well as for his wife who had left the country to spend a month in Mozambique with Heidi Baker of Iris Ministries. Despite being on a fast, Wayne served as an excellent host to us cyclists, fixing us sandwiches and all.

As we ate, things outside seemed strange to me. I noticed there weren't any people in the area. No one on any of the sidewalks. No one in the parking lot. No vehicles driving by. It felt like a ghost town. It was as if 'the Rapture' had happened.

Suddenly, a coach bus pulled in. Then another. And another, and another, and another ... Seven coach buses in all, right across from the front steps of the capitol. I watched as the bus doors opened ... and out poured girls. Teenage girls. Girl after girl after girl. I wondered, *What in the world is going on?* As I continued to watch, I noted that each girl was wearing a sash over a shoulder, like the type worn in a beauty pageant, every sash bearing the same two words. It took me a while but I was eventually able to make out the words: Girls State.

The girls were at the capitol to participate in a summer program designed to educate young women in citizenship and the workings of government. They represented high schools throughout the state of Alabama. I said to the others, "That's great. I didn't know they were coming." No one else around and then suddenly, all these girls on the front steps of the state capitol. It happened around 11:30 AM, just as we were finishing our lunch. I continued watching as the girls were handed boxed lunches. There were at least three hundred and fifty girls, perhaps as many as three hundred and eighty.

After a half hour passed I said, "Well, it's twelve o'clock." We picked up the cross and, dressed in our spandex cycling shorts and shirts, carried it across the street and up the steps, all the way to the top. We set the cross in the midst of about twenty girls who were just finishing their lunch. They asked, "What are you guys doing? What's going on?"

I said, "God sent us to pray over the state capitols, to pray for our nation, to pray for our governors and senators and schools, and everything else." They said, "That's great! We've been praying this week some too." They began asking us a lot of questions. After a few minutes, I told them, "We came to pray. That's what we're here for."

The girls started hollering at the other girls saying, "Hey! Y'all come over here! We're going to have prayer! We're going to pray!" As about three hundred girls made their way toward the cross, I said, "Well, let's grab hands and make a circle." Taking hands, we formed a circle, stretching out across the front lawn of what once served as the capitol of the Confederate States of America. However, this would not be a prayer for a return to how things used to be, but a prayer for what God is doing now … today.

Who would have believed that on a Friday afternoon when no one else was around, God would send top high school students from all over the state to have a prayer meeting with us? What are the chances of that happening? If we had provided radio stations with info, sent out flyers, and done everything we could to promote it, we couldn't have had a meeting like that. God had that meeting planned. I'm telling you, when you've heard the voice of God and you step out in faith, God will show up and confirm what you're doing.

In the middle of our prayer circle was a news cameraman who had been sent to film the Girls State delegates. I got so excited I almost forgot how to pray. I just wanted to run around and start shouting because God was in this thing. But we got to praying. We prayed for teachers. We prayed for schools. We prayed for principals. We prayed for governors, senators, and congressmen. We prayed for revival in our nation and for an outpouring of the Holy Spirit. It was awesome, all those girls praying with us.

All too soon I had to say, "Okay, we've got to go." The girls were all excited. I'm certain that when they returned to their homes and schools, every one of them remembered our prayer meeting on the steps of the state capitol. God has a way of influencing things. Wow! God did something that day. He put something in motion and every one of those girls was a part of it.

After tying up the cross to the back of the motorhome, we hopped on our bikes, shifted gears, and rode westward out of town. Our adrenaline was flowing. The Holy Ghost was flowing.

Whew! We were riding like crazy. We rode until our bodies gave out.

After setting up at an RV campground that night, we went around looking for, and found, someone with a television. I asked, "Can we watch the news tonight with you because we've been at the state capitol and the news cameras were there in our prayer circle." I figured the station would show it on the news because of all the girls praying. But as we watched, the station aired only an interview with the girls and a short interview with us; nothing about the prayer meeting.

It's telling how the media will run reports about teenage girls getting pregnant out of wedlock or about them doing drugs and all kinds of crazy things, but won't show three hundred-plus high school girls gathered at the capitol praying for their state. I tried later to obtain a copy of the video of our prayer circle but couldn't. I believe the media had some kind of bias there.

Regardless, we were off and running. There was no turning back now. We were going to keep riding and praying. The Lord said, "When you're not preaching somewhere, when the doors are not open, you just keep riding and praying." So we determined to continue our ride of faith to pray over state capitols ... to see God move ... to see revival come to America.

8

Revivals Begin

I believe God was changing my calling to fulfill the office of prophet and evangelist simultaneously. When I preached revival in churches, it was in something of an evangelistic office; but when on the road cycling, prophesying and declaring the words of God over the land and state capitols, it was in more of a prophetic office.

While praying in front of the state capitol in Montgomery, Alabama, our motorhome was parked across the street from the church where Martin Luther King, Jr. had preached. I didn't know when we left town that we would be on the same route as the famous civil rights march of 1965 — the Selma To Montgomery National Historic Trail. The march occurred a little before my time as I was not very old then. In Selma we had opportunities to see and read things that helped us realize the great struggles that took place back then. I believe God was giving us a heart for those struggles. God was also opening the door for me.

Wayne returned to Florida as the rest of us returned to

Tennessee to take a break from cycling for a while. I already had revival services scheduled for a church in Haleyville, Alabama. The pastor's wife, Sister Ruth, was at the Christian television station in Savannah the night I preached at the share-a-thon. An awesome singer and worship leader, she had a lot of family members with her that night. In fact, it was her nephew who got saved after his grandfather prayed over him and the Holy Spirit touched him. After the Spirit fell upon that place, Ruth said to me, "We've been looking for the person to come preach revival for us, and I believe you're it. I need to talk to my husband David, but I believe that you're it."

So after a short break, I returned to Haleyville to preach revival. Pastor David was connected with Faith Tabernacle in Florence, Alabama, where a pastors conference was scheduled to take place in a couple of weeks. We looked forward to the possibility of attending that conference. In the meantime, God would break out in an awesome way at Haleyville. The house was packed every night and people were getting touched by the Holy Spirit.

I remember one lady separated from her husband and hungry for God. The Lord touched her so powerfully one night that she had to be helped out of the church. Although she stumbled some, we thought she was able to walk and so left her alone outside. When we returned later, we found her lying on the ground. We picked her up and put her in Sister Ruth's car to take her home but didn't know where she lived. Pastor David and I decided to drive her truck to her home so she wouldn't have to return for it the following day. Her nine-year old son gave us directions as she was too drunk in the Spirit to do or say anything. Sister Ruth followed us.

Arriving at the woman's home, we carried her from Sister Ruth's car into her living room where we laid her on the couch. As we were leaving, Pastor David said, "Man, I don't know about all this. I just want to have revival. I don't know about carrying people home." I said, "Pastor, you wanted revival. This is part of it. We should be rejoicing that we have the opportunity to carry people home that are so filled with and drunk in the Holy Spirit that they cannot walk on their own."

Revival is work. A lot of work. But it's awesome when God's presence and power comes onto the scene. I think about the disciples when Jesus told them to feed the five thousand. What did they have? Two fish and five loaves of bread. Jesus told them to have the people sit down in groups of fifty. We're talking five thousand men *plus* women and children. Can you imagine twelve men, maybe a few others also, separating the groups into fifty apiece? That's a lot of work. Can you imagine catering to all those people? Twelve men catering to one hundred people would be a bit of a work. Twelve men catering to five thousand people would be a tremendous amount of work. And what if the total number of people was actually closer to ten thousand?

Yet, it turned out to be not so much work for the disciples because Jesus kept giving them bread and fish to set before the people. Can you imagine? Right before your eyes the food just keeps multiplying as you take your basket to one group of fifty, then another, and another, over and over again as the miracle of bread and fish keeps happening. Before you know it, thousands have been fed and it turned out to be not quite as much work because of all the miracles that happened while serving the Lord.

Revival is work. But in the midst of revivals, miracles will keep you going. Seeing God's hand at work keeps you going. It empowers you to not stop. We saw miracles happen in Haleyville. People got saved and got right with God. They laid out under the power of God, then went out and testified. It was awesome.

Pastor David and Sister Ruth took a break from revival in Haleyville to attend the pastor's conference in Florence. I was able to go as well. The pastor of Faith Tabernacle provided free food and lodging for all pastors and ministers attending the conference. It was awesome. There was a houseful in that church each day;

maybe five to seven hundred pastors and ministers with their wives, as well as other people. Eddie Lawrence, Pastor Johnny Sloan, and Sister Diane Sloan (Johnny's wife) were scheduled to preach Tuesday, Wednesday, and Thursday. I wasn't aware the pastor had obtained a copy of my Brownsville testimony and showed it to his congregation.

As it turned out, Brother Sloan had to leave the conference a day early. Since he was scheduled to preach at the Thursday evening service, they moved Diane to that service and Pastor Eddie to the afternoon service, leaving the morning spot open. I was asked to take that spot. I thought to myself, *What a challenge!* I could feel the Spirit of God coming over me, but I was also thinking, *Man, here I am having pastored just a few years. What do I know about speaking to a bunch of pastors?* Yet, it's not *what* we know but *Who* we know that empowers us. Hallelujah!

That morning, I preached about King David and how, in a time when kings went out to war, he stayed home. While on the rooftop one evening, he saw his neighbor's wife Bathsheba bathing and, instead of focusing on something else, lusted after her and continued to lust after her until he committed adultery with her. He thought he could hide the affair by arranging for her husband to be killed, but God sent a prophet to expose him. As it is written, "your sin will find you out." If we sit around the house taking it easy and don't pursue God, we can easily fall into sin.

As I continued to preach about King David, the Holy Spirit came in. I preached through my entire allotted hour. Brother Eddie got up and said, "Brother Bill, just keep preaching. Don't stop. Just keep ministering." But then the pastor stood up and said, "Wait just a minute. We want to take up an offering for this brother." He put up a basket and said, "Anybody that wants to give, just come up and give." After they had given, I continued preaching for a few more minutes.

As I ended my message, I prayed and asked, "Who wants the anointing? We've got to go after God. We can't be idle. We have to pursue God. We've got to have revival." A wave of pastors came forward. I laid hands on them and saw the power of God move on them. The fire of God laid them out on the floor. Hearts were changed and lives recommitted to serving God. It was an exciting time. I thought, *Man, God's really moving and opening doors now, opening the doors that no man can shut and shutting the doors that no man can open.*

While driving back to Tennessee to rest a few days before returning to Haleyville to preach more revival, I counted the offering. $2,500. Praise God. The Bible says that God shall supply all of your needs according to His riches in glory by Jesus Christ. And He had done just that for me. Hallelujah! Amen.

Following the meetings in Haleyville, my cycling team traveled to Indianapolis for a three-day World Assemblies of God Meeting. From there we rode our bikes to Columbus, Ohio, and prayed outside the state capitol. We also went inside. It was late and no one was there. I mean, no one. We began to sing "Amazing Grace." Our notes echoed throughout the entire place. The Holy Ghost was in the House. It was awesome.

Next, we drove to Virginia to visit some friends in Blacksburg, then on to Richmond to preach at a friend's church. Since we were so close to Ashland, we drove up to check out Campmeeting at Calvary Campground. Revival meetings there would run about eight weeks at a time. Rooms were available on a first-come, first-served basis. Alternatively, you could camp out. There were different ministers about every three days and at least two meetings per day. Breakfast and lunch were free, supported only by offerings.

Sister Ruth Ward Heflin, who was overseeing the ministry her father had started, was battling cancer at the time. I saw her only once during the week I was there. She passed away a few weeks later. Sister Ruth was an awesome woman of God who had traveled and preached all over the world.

I was back in Richmond when I heard about the

arrangements for her funeral and it worked out so that our team could attend. Pastors from all over the world were there. Wow, how she impacted people in sixty years.

I went by her casket three different times. I said, "Lord, if there is any anointing left here, I receive it." I know that may sound strange, but there was enough anointing left in the bones of Elisha to raise the dead.

After that, my team and I returned to Pensacola. From there, my son and I rode to many different locations including the Florida state capital. A friend named Keith, who I had met in Haleyville, was now driving the motorhome for us.

We were at the capitol in Tallahassee praying as the votes for U.S. presidential candidates George W. Bush and Al Gore were being re-tallied in a historic recount. Inside the capitol was a chapel with a historical record of Christianity in Florida beginning with the time of the Spaniards. The last section of that record cited the importance of other religions in the state, which was rather sad to see. But it was awesome to see the chapel that had been established there.

From Tallahassee, we drove the motorhome down to Dade City to visit of a pastor friend of mine named Tim who I had met at the pastors conference in Florence, Alabama, a few weeks earlier. He had been to the Brownsville Revival and seen my New Year's Eve testimony. I preached revival at his inner city church for a couple of weeks. Denise and the girls met up with us there. Together, we traveled all the way down to John Pennekamp State Coral Reef Park at the top of the Florida Keys. I believed God wanted me to ride out to the end of the Keys, put a stake in the ground at Key West, and pray over the land. In fact, God had spoken to me about putting a stake in each of the four corners of the United States.

We stayed at the park a couple days and swam in the ocean before my son and I began the hundred-mile ride out to the end of the Keys. God opened doors for us to stay at an Assembly of God Church in Key West under the care of our friend Pastor Ernie. It was around Thanksgiving. We carried the cross through the city amidst all that was going on at the time.

There were a lot of homosexuals in Key West and a strong "gay" influence with a large gay church, a gay mayor, and various other gay-related things. There was something of a carnival atmosphere in the air. A lot of things that I don't care to mention happened while we were there praying and carrying the cross through town. We met a lot of runaway teenagers and many homeless people. Pastor Ernie had a heart for those people.

A number of out-of-state believers came down to Key West to host a turkey dinner for the homeless. It was great having my family with me and being able to participate in that. We prayed over the town. We drove a stake into the flower bed in front of the church and declared God's kingdom and revival in the land.

In January of the following year, I traveled with my dad to St. Croix in the U.S. Virgin Islands where he was serving as construction superintendent over a nighttime crew at an oil refinery. Dad had asked whether I knew of any men at the churches where I preached "who wanted to work for about six weeks and make some good money." I said, "Let me work on it."

After giving it some thought, I came up with an idea. I called a bunch of my friends and said to them, "I have an all expense paid mission trip to the Virgin Islands for six weeks. All you have to do is work when you get there, but you will have about five hundred construction workers to minister to." Ten friends from different churches took me up on it and went down to work the six weeks at the refinery. I arrived in St. Croix about a week before they did and stayed in a condo with my dad, mother, and cousin for a total of about eight weeks.

The men lived in what is called a "man camp" consisting basically of a large metal building with dividers serving as walls for rooms. From within their "rooms" men couldn't see one another, yet could hear every little noise that was made.

I had the opportunity to witness and preach in churches as well as become a "camp daddy." My duties included picking up workers from the airport, getting them checked in, taking them to safety orientation, handling their complaints, making sure they were happy and didn't go home early, and returning them to the airport upon completion of their assignments.

The job also presented me with the potential of having to deal with workers who stayed out late drinking and got into serious trouble. But that was an opportunity to minister. And it was a relief compared to the first jobs I had such as standing on a narrow platform a hundred feet or so above the ground against a strong wind while loosening bolts on a man hole cover, or trying to loosen bolts with a large impact gun without kicking up any sparks in an environment where sparks are about the last thing anyone wants to see.

God was opening a lot of doors for me both evangelistically and prophetically. I got to preach and pray for people on different islands, including St. John. And I was able to save up some money. I had a chance to stay for another job when I received word that my grandmother who had been sick with cancer had passed away.

Both my grandmother and grandfather (who had already passed on) had a big impact on my life. I spent a lot of time with them off and on. They always took me to church and told me about Jesus. If I remember correctly, my parents and I flew out from the island the very next day so we could be at the funeral in time. I had the privilege of preaching at Grandmother's funeral, along with my cousin Randall who is also a preacher.

Eight weeks of work on the island had provided me with enough finances to get back on the road again. God had supplied my needs. Sometimes, we must take work that we ordinarily wouldn't. And sometimes, God just supernaturally opens doors.

I believe God had a ministry for those ten men and myself to do on the Virgin Islands. It was great. The ten guys from the states had never had an opportunity like that before. It really touched and changed their lives. Especially the life of Pastor Vince from Grand Junction, Tennessee. Vince had partnered with me during the twenty-five weeks of revival in Bolivar. He said, "I prayed with one man who was missing his family. Then I went in the room and started crying because I was missing my own family. I had never been away from them this long."

The experience gave those ten men a heart for what it means to be out on the road, in the field, away from family. It's not an easy road, but when God calls us to do something, we can do it. The apostle Paul wrote, "I can do all things through Him who strengthens me" (Philippians 4:13).

In returning to the states, it seemed God had plans for me to head out to the Pacific Northwest and begin a ride there. The basic plan was to start somewhere near the Pacific Ocean and ride south to the state capitols at Olympia, Washington, and Salem, Oregon, before turning eastward for Helena, the capital of Montana, and continuing on to the capitals of North and South Dakota. Prior to beginning the ride, I would drive to the tip of Washington, drive a stake into the ground, and pray over the state and the nation. This time, I would be taking my family with me.

After making preparations, we set out on our journey. We traveled along a number of routes used by pioneers who had ventured into the Wild West via wagon train decades ago. We eventually made it to Seattle, Washington, where we learned that the tip of the state was on the Olympic Peninsula … occupied by the Makah People.

After spending a few days in the city, we set out for the Peninsula. It would be dark before we got there. Driving late at night and with only our headlights to light the way, we discovered that the Strait of Juan de Fuca Highway wasn't exactly designed for a rig like ours. With the windows of the motorhome open we could hear water crashing against a rocky shoreline below. Had we known what sort of road we were on, it might have terrified us. We would find out later that it was very narrow with steep drop-offs and cliffs.

We made it to Neah Bay on the Makah reservation around midnight. Behind our motorhome was a trailer bearing the words "Pray for America." As we pulled into the parking lot of a general store, two guys were standing outside. I asked, "Where's The Assembly of God church in town?" One of them, a young man, said, "I used to go there. It's right down the road and around this block. Did you come to preach?" I said, "Well, whatever God wants to do, that's what we want to do, but we came to pray."

We found the church right where the young man said it was and parked the motorhome in its parking lot for the night. As we got ready to sleep, we could hear a bell on a buoy out in the bay. It bonged all night long. We also heard a lot of barking out on the water. We found out later that it was from sea lions. No fish had been brought in during the day by charter or commercial fishermen and the sea lions were making some noise about it. Despite the ruckus, there was a peace in the atmosphere as we slept.

Early the next morning, there was a knock on our door. I opened it to find a man who greeted me with, "Hello. How are you doing? Did you come to preach?" I said, "Well, we'll do whatever God wants us to do." Turns out he was a deacon at the church. I got to talking with the brother and learned that the church didn't have a pastor. They had just voted one in but it would be a couple weeks before he arrived. I told him my family came to pray. He said, "Okay. I'm going to go talk with the tribe and see where we can go pray."

I didn't know Reservations were Sovereign Nations and that we needed permission to pray on the reservation. But it was good that protocol was taking place. Our spiritual brother did what he could for us before he had to leave for work. He was able to get us permission to pray and told us where we could go to do so. In fact, he drove me to a spot overlooking the Pacific Ocean, where waves could be seen crashing upon the shoreline, and asked, "Would this be a good place?" I responded, "This is a great place." He said, "Well, I have permission from the tribal counsel and we'll come here and pray." I said, "Great."

The following morning, we drove our motorhome on about four to six miles of dirt and paved roads all the way out to the end of the peninsula. Upon arrival, we found our brother and some other native people waiting there for us. This was our first real contact with Native American people and our first experience of being on a reservation. We stood there and prayed and recited the scripture, "If My people who are called by My name will humble themselves, and pray and seek My face, and turn from their wicked ways, then I will hear from heaven, will forgive their sin and will heal their land."

It was kind of foggy, but we could see eagles flying overhead. As the fog began to lift, we could see ocean waves crash onto the shore, and little islands out a ways. With our Native American brothers and sisters gathered there with us, we drove a stake into the ground. We prayed and asked God for an awakening. We asked Him to bring revival to America and to pour out His Spirit upon the land. It was just an awesome time together. It would also be the beginning of another journey.

My family and I lingered on the reservation for a couple days. We watched a dance and a cultural exchange between native kids who had come down from Canada. We participated in some of their dances. We then took to the road.

Denise and the girls followed my son and me as we rode our bikes from the reservation down to Olympia, Washington, where we prayed over the state capitol. We then cycled south to Salem, Oregon, and prayed over the state capitol there before riding eastward through Oregon. We put our bikes up at Redmond (just north of Bend) and from there drove to Hungry Horse, Montana, a short distance from the west entrance to Glacier National Park. We took a day of rest there, then got an early start the next morning in cycling through the middle of the park on Going-To-The-Sun Road. Much of the road was fairly easy to cycle but then became rather steep. By the time we reached Logan Pass, my son and I had climbed some 3,500 feet on our bikes. Having reached the top, it was all downhill to the other side. We were able to pick up some serious speed en route to the eastern side of the park.

As the two of us cycled *through* the park, Denise and the girls drove the motorhome on what I thought was a bypass *around* the park. I would find out later that the road they were on was about as bad as ours. But my wife did a great job navigating the 38-foot motorhome with 14-foot trailer all the way.

Upon meeting up in St. Mary on the other side of the park, I said to Denise, "Well, we need to drive back that way." She said, "I'm not driving back that way." I said, "That's okay, I'll drive." She replied, "I'm not even *riding* back that way."

As it turns out, no vehicle over thirty feet in length is supposed to be on that road; but because I didn't see any sign that said so, I had told Denise to go that way. The girls had taken note of how close the motorhome came to the edge of the mountain. To them, it looked like the wheels were going off the cliff and they had been having a serious prayer meeting about it. So we decided to stay put in St. Mary until we came up with a plan. Besides, we were almost out of food and money.

We needed something to happen. I believed God would provide. How, I didn't know. But He was about to show up again and do great and mighty things. Praise the Lord!

9

Camp Meeting

As we sat in our motorhome in St. Mary on the eastern edge of Glacier National Park, I pondered the situation. *There are no big churches or towns around this area and we are running out of money. Maybe the best thing for us to do would be to go north to Canada. Maybe there we can find a pretty good-sized town and pull into a church. Perhaps God wants to provide for us that way. When we pull in there, maybe they'll open the doors for us to minister or something.*

So that weekend, we took a trip up north into Canada and found a nice-sized church. We parked the RV outside and went inside. But nothing really happened. Aside from meeting some nice people and being invited to lunch, there were no open doors for us.

On our way back down to St. Mary, I asked God, *What do we do now? We're a long ways from any opportunity for ministry.* Or so I thought.

I called a friend, Dr. Larry Martin, who was ministering at the Brownsville Revival School of Ministry, and asked him to pray for us. I said, "I don't know what's going on. We're stuck up here in Montana and there's no money, no gas, and not much food left. We need some help." He said he would pray and that he would call a pastor friend in Gillette, Wyoming, to let him know we would be coming through town. He figured when we got to Gillette — which was several hundred miles away — we might have an opportunity to preach and possibly receive an offering.

Now, I had this figured out in my mind, how everything was going to work out. But God was about to teach me an awesome lesson. Like it says in Isaiah 55: "My thoughts are not your thoughts, nor are your ways My ways ... For as the heavens are higher than the earth, so are My ways higher than your ways and My thoughts than your thoughts."

The following morning, my family woke up to snow on the ground. I thought, *How are we going to start riding bicycles with this snow on the ground?* Suddenly, I thought back to 1986 and my ride across America. I remembered that about thirty miles down the road was a small town called Browning ... on the Blackfeet Indian Reservation. Since we could no longer afford to stay at the RV park in St. Mary, I decided we should head for Browning. So we loaded up the motorhome and took off.

One of the lessons I had learned on my journey of life is that if things aren't going right, supplies aren't coming in, and it just seems like I'm not hearing from heaven, there are two things I ask the Lord. First, I ask Him if there's something in my life that's stopping His flow. Like it says in Psalm 139: "Search me, O God, and know my heart: try me, and know my thoughts: and see if there be any wicked way in me, and lead me in the way everlasting" (KJV).

Sometimes when things are not going right, there may be something we did that offended the Holy Spirit. We may have done something or gone in a direction that's not pleasing to God. I believe that is always the first thing we need to find out. We may need to repent, seek the Lord, and say, "God, if there's something in my life that's stopping your flow, show me so I can turn away from it."

The second thing I do after searching my heart and bringing about any needed correction is to say, "Okay, God. What are you trying to teach me from this?" Sometimes, God is quiet when He's testing us. "Lord, what do you want me to learn out of this? How can I turn this situation around?"

I believe that a true believer does not fail God's tests; he simply keeps taking them until he passes. Any man or woman of God that goes after God is going to have tests along the way. God will want to see if you're going to be faithful. If you're going to continue on in a task that He's given you, even when things don't look so good, you have to go back to that moment when you heard His word.

I heard a word from God in my bath tub in Sidonia, Tennessee, telling me to get up and ride to state capitols. If you are going to walk by faith, you need to hear a word from God that will keep you going all along the way.

So, my family and I drove on down to Browning, a Native American community with only one grocery store. We parked our motorhome and trailer out front of the store and went inside to get some hot dogs and a can of chili—a pretty cheap meal to cook in our motorhome.

As Denise was preparing our food, there came a knock at the door. *Bam, bam, bam!* I opened the door to find an elderly man of maybe seventy years old. He said, "Hello, my name is Tiny Man."

I looked at him and thought, *Tiny Man? He's about six foot, seven inches.* The best I can remember, he was several inches taller than I was. A very robust, strong-looking man.

He said, "I saw your *Pray for America* trailer back there. I also saw your license plate is from Tennessee. I just wanted to say hello and that I am a Christian and I married a woman from Tennessee a few years back." I said to him, "Come on in the motorhome!"

Man, talk about a breath of fresh air. We really hadn't had any good fellowship with other Christians for a while. It felt like we had been out on our own there, just going along, and then suddenly, God sends someone to minister to us.

We shared with Tiny Man about our journey. He said, "Praise the Lord! You know what? I got saved about four years ago and there are four full gospel churches in this town. Between the four, I'm going to church somewhere every night." It was Tuesday. He continued, "You know what? I'm going to go contact my friends here, Fred and Phyllis. They have a house church tonight. Why don't ya'll just come over there and visit at the house church?" I said, "Man, that'll be great!"

Tiny Man left to tell Fred and Phyllis about us and then returned to show us the way over to the house church. And yes, it was literally a house church with the center wall cut out to add more room. There were about forty people in attendance that night. A few more could have maybe fit in there. We were able to say hello to Fred and Phyllis and visit with them for a couple minutes before Brother Fred had to get up and lead worship.

The music that night was like old time camp music. They had a PA system and guitars with amps cranked up. Man, they were really going after Jesus. I got so excited and started clapping because we were in a house full of believers who believed in revival and were expecting a move of God. I started dancing, and jumping up and down. My wife gave me a little elbow and said, "You need to settle down a little bit. These people don't know us." But it was hard for me not to get excited because I was just so glad to be around fellow Christians.

Everyone in that house was Native American except my wife, my girls, my son, and me. We definitely stood out, but that was okay.

After the worship, Sister Phyllis got up to speak. She encouraged people, shared a few things, and spoke about the

Lord. She then looked at me and said, "Brother Bill, I sure did enjoy your little dance. Why don't you come up here and preach to us tonight." I gave my wife a little elbow back and said to her, "See what a dance will get ya?" I then went up to preach.

See, when you're 'out there' and want to worship the Lord, or you're just excited about God, you never know what might happen. That little dance might have been just the thing that opened the door to Sister Phyllis. God was watching our reactions in that place. When you feel the Spirit of God come upon you to dance, shout, clap your hands, or run, just obey Him. As we move in the Spirit, as we hear God and obey, it opens doors that might not otherwise be opened.

It's like in 2 Kings 13 where Elisha is lying on his bed, about to die, when Joash, king of Israel, enters the room and says, "You know, we're surrounded by Syrians and we need some help here." So Elisha says to him, "Okay, take this arrow and shoot it out the window." [slightly paraphrased]

Now, that seems like a real strange thing, to take an arrow and shoot it out the window. If the enemy was out there, one arrow would just make them mad; it wouldn't help anything. However, as soon as the king shot that arrow out the window, the word of the Lord came to Elisha and he said to Joash, "You shall strike the Syrians at Aphek until you have destroyed them." As soon as Joash carried out the prophetic act, God moved and gave him a word from heaven.

I believe that as soon as that dance came to me, God moved and opened a door. After I preached that night, Pastor Fred said to me, "Please stay another day and preach to us again." So we spent the night in town and I preached again the following night.

As Browning was one of the poorest towns in the U.S., every mission board would have said it was not a good place to raise money for mission work. In my mind as well it did not seem like a good place to raise money. Yet, in the two days we were there, God provided us with $400, which not only met our need for food and gas but was enough to get us to the next place we needed to get to: Gillette, Wyoming.

God was showing me that my provision is not about the big church or outward appearances. "I can supply your needs out of the least of these. It's Me that is your supply, not man." Don't drive by looking at the big churches, thinking, *Oh, if I could preach there, or if I could just get with a millionaire or the right person, I could just do this*. No, it's God who is the supplier of our needs. And He can supply anywhere. If the Lord could command ravens to bring food to the prophet Elijah while he hid at the Brook Cherith (see 1 Kings 17:1-6), how much more can He supply our needs!

Just before my family and I left town, Pastor Fred invited me to come back later that year and preach at the 35th annual camp meeting on the reservation. I thought, *What an honor for me, this Tennessee hillbilly to come back and preach on the reservation. God is truly doing something in our hearts with Native American people.* "Yes, I'd be glad to come back and preach here on the reservation for the camp meeting," I said. "But we're going to head east first. We have a few more cities to pray over. And then I'm going to take my family home and give them a break. I will find a couple of ministers to come back out here with me and preach this camp meeting on the reservation."

"Great!" said Pastor Fred. We prayed together. Then Denise and the girls got in the motorhome, my son and I mounted our bicycles, and together we head southward for Helena, the state capital of Montana.

It took us a couple of days to get to Helena. We had a prayer meeting at the capitol, then put the bikes up and continued on to northeastern Wyoming.

In Gillette, we met with the pastor of the First Assembly of God which took up an offering for us. In addition, Brother Larry had sent up $150. The combined offerings were enough to keep us going.

We traveled into North Dakota where we got in some cycling before camping out in Bismarck, the state capital. We then cycled and RV'd our way down to Pierre, South Dakota, where we prayed over the state capitol there and had an awesome time meeting some great Christians.

Before returning home, we spent a week in eastern South Dakota with the Crevier family. Every year, the Creviers hosted a week-long camp meeting on their ranch. They had daily and nightly meetings. People came from all over. There were tents all over the place. It was just awesome.

After returning home to give my family a break, the pastor of Bible Believer's Church in Dresden, Tennessee, asked me to come and preach. So I went up there to minister, spending the weekend with my friends Cheryl and Charles ('Charlie') Penick.

Cheryl had previously visited my church in Sidonia and prayed for us, but I hadn't met her husband until now. I found him to be an awesome man. I said to him, "I'm fixin' to go on this thirty-day trip. First, we're going to the Blackfeet Reservation in Browning, Montana, to preach … then on to Roosevelt, Utah … and then we're coming back home. Would you like to go? I feel like maybe you're one of the men who should go with me."

I already had another guy lined up to go with me: Brother Ron, a minister friend down in Mississippi. I thought that if Charlie wanted to go, the three of us would make a good crew for the trip.

Charlie attended a Baptist church for the most part, but he also checked out other churches. He had retired from working as a construction pipe fitter in a job that involved a lot of traveling. He had planted a garden in his yard, was putting up some buildings for some of his children or grandchildren to live in, and was looking forward to retiring on his farm and taking it easy. As I was leaving his home Monday morning, I said, "If you want to go, let me know. I'm leaving on Wednesday."

The following night, Charlie called me and said, "You

know what? I'm gonna go. I'm going to sow this time into God. I'm gonna give Him thirty days and then I'm gonna come back and I'm gonna take care of my garden and my kids and I'm just going to enjoy retirement." I said, "That's good."

So Wednesday morning, Miss Cheryl brought Charlie down to where Brother Ron and I had arranged to meet him. We loaded up our vehicle and started out on our journey. First stop: International House of Prayer (IHOP), Kansas City, Missouri.

I said to my companions, "Man, I haven't been to IHOP. I think we'll go by there and just visit that place a bit and get filled up, get in that anointing, and just let the presence of the Lord come on us. We'll get some prayer there, and pray, and then we'll be ready for our trip." After spending the night with some friends just south of town, we went in for the IHOP experience. I thought we might spend an hour or two, but it ended up being more like six to eight hours. It was a pretty interesting time for Charlie because he had never been in an environment like that before.

IHOP was founded in the spirit of the tabernacle of David (see 1 Chronicles 23:1-5; 25:1-7) with worship teams ministering before the Lord seven days a week, twenty-four hours a day. In 2001 the ministry was housed in a structure that looked like a specially-made office building with a large sanctuary. You could just lie around on the floor if you wanted to. There were pillows against the walls, and chairs here and there. You could just enter in and make yourself at home, 'marinate' in the anointing, and feel the Lord's presence while walking around, praying, dancing, whatever you felt like doing.

Brother Charlie felt God's presence come over him the moment he walked into the prayer room. He told me later, "I was sitting in my chair and I leaned my head down on the chair in front of me to just kind of think about what was going on. After a few minutes, maybe ten or fifteen minutes, I looked back up and there was a whole different worship team and I never heard the music change! I'm wondering, *Where in the world did these people go? Did the Rapture happen or something?"* It really blew his mind. He said, "What is going on in this place?" What he didn't know was that every two hours a different worship team leader takes the stage and begins to perform, allowing the previous worship team to exit and the next team to enter, get set up, and begin performing without the music ever really stopping. Charlie said, "I'm going to the break room."

As Charlie sat in the break room, drinking some coffee, a lady and her son sat down and began conversing with him. The woman said, "Would you mind if we prayed?" He thought, *Well, no, that's probably not going to hurt anything.* So he said, "Go ahead." As she started praying, a whole gang of people came around and prayed over him a few minutes. After they finished praying, the woman asked him, "Can I tell you what I saw?" He's thinking, *Saw? What do you mean, "saw"? How do you see something when you're praying?* The woman had seen in the Spirit. She said to Charlie, "I saw Jesus take your heart out of you and put His heart in you. And it was so big that it made your T-shirt stick out." She continued, "It's for the Native American people."

Now, that really touched Charlie because the woman didn't know we were headed to Montana to visit the Blackfeet people. God was doing something inside of him.

When you take mission trips, when you go out on the road, when you get outside of your comfort zone, there is no limit to what God can do. It's awesome. And it's been a tremendous blessing for me to take people out to where God is moving, that their lives might be changed by the anointing … by the Word of God … by prophetic words … by impartation.

Continuing westward, Ron, Charlie and I reached Sturgis, South Dakota, home to the annual Sturgis Motorcycle Rally. I had wanted to visit Sturgis during this time of year to see what God might doing in the place and if anyone was doing any outreach with so many bikers coming in from all over the U.S. It was estimated that upwards of six hundred thousand people would come through town during the week of the rally.

We were able to camp at the Assembly of God church in town; which was rather providential because all the church people had left town and didn't want anyone camping out on their property, but an Assemblies of God missionary/evangelist who happened to be camped there gave us permission to park our motorhome for the night.

Personally, I thought it would have been a great week for the church to be doing outreach. They could have invited ministry teams to come in and reach out to those that God was bringing to their community. But that's another story.

We spent two days in Sturgis, seeing what went on, traveling about the area some. The evangelist clued us in on some things. We met a guy known as Biker Mike who used to be in biker gangs and had a big tent set up where he preached the gospel all week long. We heard testimonies from a lot of folk. It was awesome what God was doing there. He was reaching out to people. There is no place too dark for Jesus to come into.

Just before leaving town for Gillette, Wyoming, where I was scheduled to preach the coming Sunday, the wife of the missionary/evangelist spoke with Charlie. He had been telling her about his visit to IHOP. She said to him, "I have something to tell you, too. God wants to use you in a mighty way and He's going to do great things through you, but there's something that comes in a round can or a bottle that you're going to have to deal with before God really moves in your life." Well, Charlie liked to dip Skoal. But the woman had no way of knowing that since he didn't have any in his pocket. God was getting Charlie's attention. He was reading Charlie's mail.

Charlie returned to the motorhome more spiritually messed up than he was before. "Now God's speaking even more to me!" he said. It was amazing to see what God was doing in his life. What God was doing in all three of our lives actually.

In Gillette, I preached two nights of revival and got Charlie involved in ministry. He served as a "catcher," catching people that might fall under the presence of God. He also prayed for people. At the Sunday night service, he stood before the congregation and gave a testimony. Afterwards, I called Cheryl who had been praying for us. I said to her, "Man, Charlie's just about preaching now. God's really touching him and moving in his life."

It's the sort of thing you want to see happen. God will minister to you and then raise you up to minister to others. It's awesome. And this wasn't anywhere near the end of things for us, but only the beginning of more yet to come.

We eventually made it to the Blackfeet Reservation where Fred and Phyllis blessed us and treated us wonderfully, feeding us every day. We had a week-long revival meeting in which I preached the gospel and saw people's lives touched by God. We had community fellowship meals together. It was great.

And God was doing to Charlie exactly what the woman at IHOP had prophesied: He was taking out Charlie's heart and replacing it with His heart for the Native American people ... for Fred and Phyllis and the Blackfeet people.

After spending time with the Blackfeet, my two friends and I went down to Roosevelt, Utah, where I was scheduled to preach a three-day revival. People from the Ute Reservation about seven miles to the south came up to get involved.

The first night of revival was on a Friday and man, things were just dead. I mean, nothing was going on. It seemed like the Spirit wasn't moving. In talking with Ron and Charlie later that night, I said, "You know what? We ought to just load this motorhome up and head out of here. This place is dead and these people are not interested in revival. We need to go." Brother Ron said, "You know what? I think we ought to just fast tomorrow and see what happens; just give God an opportunity to move here." So I said, "Okay, we'll seek the Lord even harder. We'll ask God to move." So we agreed to fast the following day. Guess what happened.

When you fast and seek the Lord, God will show up. On the second night, the power of God came down through the church sanctuary almost like a mighty rushing wind. The Holy Ghost swept into that place and began touching people's lives. People were lined up all over the sanctuary floor, praying. Some were falling out, hitting the ground under God's presence.

At one point, I was all the way out in the foyer, beyond the swinging doors leading into the sanctuary, praying for people when suddenly, the foyer doors just busted open, out flew Pastor Dee, and down to the floor he went. Looking over, I saw that he was slain in the Spirit. Later, he said to me, "I told God, 'I'm not taking no courtesy fall.'" And he hadn't. God just touched him and knocked him through those doors and out onto the floor. No one else touched him.

Our three-day revival wound up being seventeen days of signs, wonders and miracles. Demons manifested and were cast out.

Among those showing up to the revival was Brother Steve, a man who had been away from God and was angry and bitter at the Lord for having to be on oxygen and confined to a wheelchair. Doctors and nurses didn't like him. Most people in town didn't like him. Pastor Dee, however, had befriended him, prayed for him, and invited him to church.

One night, during the altar call for salvation, Brother Steve wheeled himself up to the front and gave his life to Jesus. Others and myself then gathered around him and began to pray for him. As we did, he pulled the oxygen mask from his face. A group of teenagers from the Native church and some Ute people then gathered around him and prayed with us. We prayed and prayed. Eventually, Steve got himself up out of that motorized wheelchair and walked around the sanctuary. God did a miracle in his life that night. Many other miracles occurred during those seventeen nights of revival as well.

One morning during this revival, I saw Charlie sitting outside the motorhome beneath some trees. I could tell he was contemplating what God was doing. He looked up to the sky, kind of shook his head, then looked down at the ground and shook his head again, as if he was asking, *God, what are you doing?*

Man, if you'll give God an opportunity, He will blow your mind. Our minds cannot comprehend the things God wants to do.

After a while, Charlie entered the motorhome and said to me, "Brother Bill, I know what you're supposed to do. I'm fixin' to have to go home. My brother's gonna come pick me up. This has gone longer than we thought, which is great, but I got paperwork I need to sign for my retirement. I gotta go back and take care of some stuff. But *you* need to load people up and take them on thirty-day trips 'cause you have messed my life up! You have changed my life!"

Actually, it wasn't me. It was the Holy Spirit. It was God. The Lord needs people who will make themselves available to do His will. God had chosen Charlie for a special assignment—a ministry, in fact—that Charlie would soon come to realize and carry out.

Charlie would go back home and plow his garden under. He would then get himself a cargo trailer bearing the words "Native American Ministries." He would load food and clothes into that trailer and return to the Blackfeet with his wife Cheryl to minister to the Native people. Those two would also help Fred and Phyllis get a church built on the reservation. God would use them in a mighty way.

Charlie's plans of retirement had been stopped. God's plan for him was not to retire, but to re-fire—to get fired up for Jesus!

It's never too late. No matter how young or old you are, God has a plan for your life.

As for me, the new adventure of ministering to Native Americans was only beginning.

One night, during the revival in Roosevelt, Wade Large

from the Ute Reservation was leading worship when suddenly, he stopped the music, looked at me, and said, "Brother Bill, I believe God wants you to go to Supai."

I got to thinking more about that when two ladies in the congregation said, "We got kinfolks down there! We got kinfolks down there!"

I'm thinking, *Where is "down there"?*

10

Down There

There I was in Roosevelt, Utah, preaching revival, when two women said, "We've got kinfolks down there! We've got kinfolks down there!" I asked myself, *Where is "down there?" What does "down there" mean? Usually, "down there" is not a good thing.*

The women said, "It's Havasupai. There's people who live in the bottom of the Grand Canyon on the Havasupai Reservation."

I thought to myself, *There's no way people live in the bottom of the Grand Canyon. I've heard and read about the Grand Canyon. I have never heard anything about people living down there.*

They said, "They live in a separate vein of the canyon. Like a tributary canyon. You have to hike, horseback, or helicopter to get down to where they live."

Wade Large had just told me that he believed God wanted me to go minister to the Supai people. So I said, "Okay, we'll see what happens."

Revival in Roosevelt, Utah, continued for seventeen days

with people getting touched by the power of God every night. A man who lived next door to the church had been down on his back for ten years. He had bolts and nuts holding his back together and had to sleep in a recliner. God healed and saved him. As a result of him getting healed, his wife and little boy gave their lives to the Lord. He was up and around the very next day helping his wife with house and yard work, and wasn't sleeping in the recliner anymore. She was very happy. If you want to reach the wife, touch the husband so that he may be healed and begin to help around the house again and become the man of God that God wants him to be.

Eventually, my two friends and I had to leave the revival in Roosevelt. After Charlie's brother came to take him home, Brother Ron and I drove south to Kingman, Arizona, to see the pastor of the Assembly of God church there. Kingman First Assembly was the church closest to the Grand Canyon that we knew of.

We met with Pastor Dan and asked him what he knew about the Havasupai. He said he had never been down to the village but that there was a woman named Olivia in his church who had previously lived there. He said, "I'll try to introduce you to Olivia. You can meet with her." He arranged for us to meet with her in the motorhome.

Olivia told us, "I've left from down there. There were drugs and different things going on and I was trying to raise my kids right. I've become a Christian. I want to serve God. So I moved up out of the canyon, up here to Kingman." She continued, "When I left there, I told God, 'I'm never going back down there again.'"

As I began to tell Olivia what happened in Roosevelt, Utah, and how God had spoken to us to go down to the Havasupai and minister to her people, she said, "Well, for that right there, I'm willing to go back down to the canyon."

It was a Wednesday afternoon. Since all Brother Ron and I

had for transportation was the big motorhome, Pastor Dan provided us a van to drive to the canyon. Olivia accompanied us. We drove out to a mesa. From there we could see the Havasupai village about a half mile down. The three of us had a time of prayer and worship there. We took communion. We asked God to open the spiritual gates and give us divine appointments. We knew He would make a way where there may not seem to be one.

The following morning, we drove the motorhome one hundred thirty miles out of Kingman to where the road dead-ends at a spot overlooking the tributary canyon about a mile wide and with a drop-off of about half a mile. Pack horses coming up the trail emerged at that spot. In fact, we learned that it's the only place in the United States where U.S. mail is carried in and out by horseback. From that location, it's about an eight-mile trek down to the Havasupai village by foot, horseback, or helicopter.

Olivia had us drop her off at the helicopter pad there. Brother Ron and I didn't know she had plans to take a chopper down to the village, so we simply let her off before driving a few hundred feet more to park the motorhome.

The two ladies at church who said, "We've got kinfolks down there!" had also said, "And we're gonna provide you with some horses to ride." Well, that sounded good. And you've got to use what God provides. But I really don't like horses. As an eighth grader, I broke my arm riding a horse. Up until that point, I had ridden bicycles, motorcycles, jet skis, snow skis, all kinds of stuff, and never really broke anything. Then I get on a horse and break my arm. Seems to me horses got a mind of their own. They do what they want to do. But I said, "You know, God, whatever it takes, whatever You supply, I'll do it."

As Brother Ron and I waited at the top of the canyon for our horses, I got my mind set on it looking just like I picture Grand Canyon National Park. There will be a mule train coming up the trail with a couple of horses tagging along and a tour guide who will help us up onto our horses and then take us safely down the trail. You need to understand, this was a switchback trail with a half-mile drop-off to the bottom. I figured we would need a guide. The switchbacks on this trail run for about half a mile before giving way to a pretty steep trail that runs straight to the bottom. And even though it's only half a mile down, it's a full mile of trail. Then, after reaching the bottom, it's about another seven miles to the village.

So there I was, having in my mind this image of a trail guide with horses or mules, when up comes a Havasupai man with two horses. I thought, *Uh-oh, that's just two. That's not a whole mule train.*

He asked, "You guys looking for the horses?" I said, "Yes." He said, "Okay, come on."

We followed him as he led the two horses back down the trail. About two switchbacks down, he said, "Okay, get on the horse. Go down the trail. Just keep following the trail. You'll wind up in the village." He then turned around and walked back *up* the trail to feed his horse. I thought he might have had some more pack horses up there. I would learn later that the Havasupai turn their horses loose on the trail to send them ahead. The horses know to go up the trail where they will be loaded with supplies before returning back down the trail.

Brother Ron and I got on our horses — that was our first mistake — and began the ride down into the canyon.

Praise God, horses have four hooves because a lot of times one or two of my horse's hooves would be sliding while the others provided some stability. However, we're only a couple of switchbacks down when next thing I know, my horse turns around on the trail, its head now facing the canyon wall as its tail hangs off the cliff, its rear hooves only inches from a drop-off of several hundred feet. To me, it looked like certain death if the horse were to back up just a bit.

I thought, *It's time now. I'm an ordained minister with the Assemblies of God Church. I've been taught how to pray. I've been a pastor. It's time for all that to kick in – for that Holy Spirit in me to kick in.* And I'll tell you how it kicks in. You pray like this: HELP! JESUS! I NEED HELP ... RIGHT NOW! *HE-E-E-E-ELP!!!*

I bet the people all the way down in the village could hear me crying out, "JESUS, I NEED HELP NOW!"

People say you don't have to get excited when you pray. But I'm telling you, when your life is in danger, you get passionate about praying. And I believe Jesus hears passionate prayers.

About the time I was crying out to Jesus, Olivia was catching a ride down in a helicopter. Ten minutes later, she's at the bottom of the canyon, walking around the village, proclaiming to the Havasupai, "The men of God are coming down! They're gonna heal the sick, raise the dead, cast out demons, cleanse the lepers! Get ready! The men of God are coming down! They're gonna preach to us!" Meanwhile, Ron and I are still up alongside the canyon wall more than seven miles away at the edge of a cliff with me yelling, "HELP! JESUS! I NEED HELP!"

Kind of strange, isn't it? Because you think, well, God sends missionaries that are qualified and trained to go into such places, right? Not really. He sends those who say, "Here I am, Lord. Use me." I may not be the most qualified. I may not be the best trained. But God's looking for those who will go, those who will hear His voice, those who will rise up and do it, trusting in Him all along the way.

Well, God answered my prayer ... though not exactly the way I wanted Him to. It wasn't long before some pack horses came up the trail, one of which hit my horse in the rear, spun him around, and got him facing in the right direction again.

Ron and I continued our journey down ... down ... down ... until finally, we reached the river bed. We then rode toward the village, taking a couple of breaks in the shade along the way.

Aside from an extra pair of blue jeans and a small

backpack, about all we had between the two of us was a box of peanut butter crackers and a gallon of water. Not a whole lot. But then, we hadn't planned on staying in the canyon all that long.

After about two and a half hours of riding and walking on a sandy trail, we finally made it to town. Our horses rocked beneath us, making it appear as though we didn't have a clue as to what we were doing. Down here, everyone rides horses, even little kids. Looking at the faces of the people as we rode into town, it seemed as though they might be thinking, *Those are supposed to be the men of God that are coming down to do something ... and they can't even ride a horse.*

God may put you in some silly situations where, in a case like this one, you might ask, "God, Why are you sending me here? Why didn't you send some cowboys? Why didn't you send somebody who can ride a horse to at least, you know, get the people's attention?" But I think God might say, "You know what? I tried to get a few cowboys. I called this one and he said, 'No, I gotta go out and do some roping on the range.'" Or, "I called this one and he said, 'No, we gotta go fix fences.'" Or, "I called this one and he said, 'No, I gotta go to a rodeo.'"

Listen, God is calling people. You or I may not be His first choice, but eventually He will get down to the one who will go, even if that person isn't already qualified because—and remember this—God is the qualifier.

In the village of Supai, there at the bottom of the canyon, green trees and other vegetation were growing. There wasn't much grass, though, because the horses eat all the grass. There were wooden houses throughout the village for its four hundred fifty-some residents. There was also a beautiful, crystal clear, blue-green water like I had never seen anywhere except maybe around some islands in an ocean. The water flowed in a stream down along the side of the village. Looking up from the bottom of the canyon, I saw rock walls that seemed about a thousand feet high, then a ledge, and above that, white rock walls extending upwards another thousand feet or so.

And so here we were, riding into town with our hands on the horns of the saddles, looking around like we didn't know anything about riding a horse. I found out later that the Havasupai have a word for white people: *ha-gooey*, meaning *white man* or, *white man riding a horse*. We were the *ha-gooeys* coming into town.

Olivia had been waiting for us at the town's helicopter pad. She said, "Come on, you guys. We've got to go pray for people." As I dismounted my horse, I felt muscles hurting in places where they had never hurt before. Have you ever been saddle sore? Well, I was saddle *sore*! When I got off that horse, I understood why cowboys walked bow-legged ... because all I could do was walk bow-legged! Everything I had was hurting. *What do you mean, "go pray for people"?* I thought. *I'm the one that needs prayer. I need crisis counseling. I almost died on the side of that mountain up there awhile ago. I'm thirsty. I'm hot. I'm tired. I'm sore. I need a place to lie down somewhere.* But Olivia insisted, "Come on, we've got to go pray for people."

You know what? It's when you least feel like praying for people that God usually moves the most and we learn that it's not about us. Man, there are times I'm so full of the Holy Spirit that I feel like I could fight hell with a water pistol. And then there are times when I'm saying, "Not today. I don't want to play. I don't want to do warfare. I don't want to fight. I don't want to do anything." Yet, it's in those times when God is ready to move in power because it's not about your feelings or emotions. You're a conduit for God to move through. He's looking for someone to move through.

I think about pastors a lot. One might be home in bed. He might be sick. Finances are going down. There may be trouble with the children. There may be issues in the church. Some bills are on the verge of not getting paid. Then someone calls and says, "Hey, could you pray for my puppy dog? She just fell off the porch awhile ago and I believe she hurt her little paw. Could you pray for her, pastor?" And he's thinking, *Pray for her? I'd like to knock her in the head, the way I'm feeling, and you're asking me to pray for a little dog?* But he quickly dismisses the thought and prays for the dog anyway, believing God, because that's what the Lord would have him do.

And so, Brother Ron and I walked through town … slowly … bow-legged … house to house. As we approached people, our restricted movements seemed to say, "Wait just a minute. When I get up there … with these slow steps … when I finally get to y'all … I'm gonna pray and God's gonna heal ya." I imagine they were looking at us, thinking, *How could God use you to do anything? You look all sore and crippled up yourself.* But you know what? In those times, God moves. Ron and I went through the village, praying for people. And God was about to open some doors for us down there in the canyon.

At one end of the village was a man in his thirties named Cleve. He had been going through a spiritual battle. As we prayed for him, God began to touch him. That would be one of our open doors. He looked at us and said, "I've got a tent set up in my backyard. You guys could stay the night in it if you want to. Spend some time with us down here." I had to tell him, "No, tonight we are going with Olivia to spend the night with her family."

As it was getting close to dusk and we understood there was a curfew for women and children because things happened there after dark, we accompanied Olivia to the home of some family members at the other end of the village. To be honest, I felt as though she was guarding us more than we were guarding her as we walked through that village.

When we arrived at her family's home, only her nephew was there. I figured the rest of the family had probably heard these white people were coming and scattered. Olivia's nephew served Ron and me each a boiled hot dog. No bun. No ketchup.

No mustard. Just a boiled hot dog. But I sure was glad to get that boiled hot dog. Man, I was hungry and my peanut butter crackers were about to run out. He also served each of us a fresh peach from a local tree.

As I happened to see the inside of their refrigerator, reality began to set in that there are people who are hurting ... people without food ... people struggling in this country. There's a mission field right here in America.

In the morning, I stepped outside and gazed at the tall, red and white walls that formed the canyon. Looking up, I thought that if we just had a roof over the thing, we'd have the world's largest building because we definitely had the walls. I began to walk around, continuing to gaze at the magnificent walls. Suddenly, I stepped into a hole and twisted my ankle. It felt as though a knife had been shoved into it. It began to swell and hurt like crazy. My body was still aching from the day before, and now I had a sprained ankle to deal with.

Down there in the canyon, people get around mostly by walking. There are no cars, no blacktop; just horses and walking on sand. I thought, *How are we gonna go pray for people? I'm bow-legged. I'm crippled. And now my ankle's sprained!* I had to find me a stick, a staff kind of like the one Moses had, to use as a prop to help me get around.

Olivia says to me, "I'm flying out today to go to a women's meeting." Since the Lord had revealed to me the previous day, about halfway down the trail, that Ron and I would be in the canyon three days and three nights, I said to her, "Oh, we got two more nights, two more days." So Ron and I walked with her to the helipad to see her off. I figured that after Olivia left, we would go down to Cleve's at the other end of the village because he had a tent and—supposedly—a couple of beds we could use.

Now, even though tourists visit Supai, they go around the village on the trail and then two miles beyond and below where there's a campground. It's very unusual for a tourist to stay in the backyard of a Supai family. But I didn't know that. I didn't know Native protocol. I just knew we were invited to stay in a backyard.

I got some ice on my ankle before Ron and I walked the half mile or so to Cleve's house. It was a sandy trail about eight or ten feet wide. I managed to find a big stick and limp along ... staff in hand ... crippled ... hurting. But I had my mind set. *I'm gonna tell somebody about Jesus. I will not let the enemy steal this opportunity and this moment from me. I'm down here in the bottom of this canyon and somebody's gonna hear about Jesus.*

Let me tell you, whatever pit you're in, whatever trial you're going through, remember to keep your eyes focused on Jesus and tell somebody about Him.

Ron and I had been praying. After walking some distance through the sand, all of a sudden the Lord came down right there. I mean, it felt like He pulled the "knife" right out of my ankle. My foot was instantly and miraculously healed. And not only that, but the saddle soreness was gone, too. Man, I was excited now. The Spirit of God had come instantaneously. I was shouting and jumping. Brother Ron looked at me and said, "I believe something's happened to you." I said, "I know it's happened!" I thought I was going to have revival right there by myself.

The Lord had spoken to me concerning the scripture, "But seek ye first the kingdom of God, and his righteousness; and all these things shall be added unto you" (Matthew 6:33 KJV). A lot of times we say, "Well, I can't do God's work until I get this straightened out. I have to take care of my marriage ... my finances ... my children." Such things can draw us away from seeking the cross. We go over here and try to fix this problem. And we go over there and try to fix that problem. And we say, "Wait, God. When I get everything fixed, I will do work for you." But God says, "If you'll just go after Me, I'll work on these problems. I'll take care of these child problems ... these money problems ... this marriage problem ... and these other things." That's not to say we should completely ignore such things or not give them any attention, but our entire focus shouldn't be on them. We have to focus on God … on the kingdom of God. As we turn our focus on the kingdom and seek after it, God will bring these other things into alignment. God will make it happen.

Ron and I made our way down to the house that Cleve was supposedly at—a house his mom and dad lived in. Inside was a little grocery store. Cleve's parents had lived on top of the canyon for a while working in grocery stores. After moving back down into the canyon, they opened a store in their living room. The store had a lot of stuff: ice cream, cold drinks, all kinds of things. I found me a Mountain Dew and drank it with the last of my peanut butter crackers. Brother Ron and I also picked up some food to eat that night.

I asked the couple, "Where is Cleve?" They said, "Well, we're not sure where he is." I said to his father Loren, "Cleve said we could stay in that tent in your backyard. Would that be okay?" Loren didn't know that Cleve had offered us the tent and he shied away from answering that question because tourists generally aren't allowed to stay in a tent in the yard of a Supai villager. But I didn't know that. He thought for a minute and said, "Okay. You guys can sleep in the tent."

So Ron and I went around to the backyard. Pulling back the door to the small, three-man dome tent, I found inside two mattresses. I'm talking real mattresses. I was praising God. You don't think about the comforts of home very much when you're at home, and it sure is good to be able to get a good night's sleep when you're out on a trail down in a canyon somewhere. That night, Ron and I crawled into the tent and got ourselves an awesome night's sleep. The air was cool and refreshing.

Upon waking up the next morning, Brother Ron and I got to talking, wondering what we were going to eat that day. We asked ourselves, *What is God going to provide today?* Just then, Loren stepped out onto the back porch of his home and called out to us, "You guys! Come in the house and eat breakfast!" I'm thinking, *Praise God! Breakfast now!*

Upon entering the house, Ron and I sat down at a little round table. Brother Loren had prepared bowls of oatmeal for us. It was awesome. And there we were, eating our oatmeal, when Loren said to us, "This morning I was taking a shower and God spoke to me. He said, 'Take care of my servants or they're gonna dust their feet off and leave here.'" He said, "Whatever we can do for you guys. You can come in our house. You can take a shower. We'll feed you some food. And you can wash your clothes. We have a washing machine. But we want you to tell us more about Jesus."

This was the chapter of a new beginning in my life. God was sending me to the mission field.

The following day, Cleve took Ron and me on a seven-mile grand tour of the canyon. He told us about the village and showed us some of the natural features, including three waterfalls. By the time we finished the hike, I knew my ankle had been totally healed.

On the third day, Brother Ron and I flew out in the helicopter — now that's the way to travel — with plans to return to the village during Thanksgiving and do an outreach. We drove south to Highway 66 and then southeast to Interstate 40.

In due time, we were on I-40, heading east through Texas, when Brother Ron got a call from his wife. It was September 11. She asked if we heard the news. We hadn't. Within minutes, we saw a huge cross off in the distance to the right. So we pulled off at Exit 112 to check it out. In the area of the cross, we found a guard shack with a small television and a security person who let us watch replays of the hijacked planes flying into the twin towers of the World Trade Center in New York City. It was awful. A lot of thoughts went through our minds about the end of times and we wondered if God might somehow use the event to bring revival to America.

As Ron and I traveled through Oklahoma, Arkansas, and

Tennessee, we heard the governor of each state come on the radio and request that people go to their local churches and pray. Apparently, the "separation of church and state" doctrine may be voided in the event of a crisis. If only all Americans knew that putting God first could avoid a lot of crises.

Having made a promise to return to the Supai Reservation, I did so in November 2001. Although Brother Ron wasn't able to go with me on that trip, many people and churches had donated food and clothing for me to take in my motorhome and trailer to the Havasupai. On my way to the reservation, Brother Wade and some of the people from Roosevelt, Utah, joined up with me. On our way down into the canyon, God gave one of the men a poem called "Supai Jesus." Brother Wade would later put it to music and the song would become very popular among the Supai people. The team stayed in Supai through Thanksgiving. We had a great outreach with many lives touched.

I thought that after leaving Supai the second time, God would have me continue praying for America and maybe visit the Havasupai only when I had time. But He had other plans. During Christmas season, my girls and I went to a winter conference at The Ramp in Hamilton, Alabama. Tommy Tenny, an awesome man of God and author of *The God Chasers*, was scheduled to be there. (Tommy has since written many more books.) Here I was in the midst of over one thousand youth praising God to loud music (including four sets of drums), when I clearly heard the Lord ask, "Would you go to the desert for one person?"

A scripture that immediately came to mind was Acts 8:26–39 where the angel of the Lord shows up and asks Philip to leave the revival in Samaria and go to the desert for one Ethiopian eunuch. Actually, the angel didn't even tell Philip why he was to go into the desert; he just told him which road to take and in what direction. But Philip didn't hesitate. Having received a *rhema* word from the Lord, he just got up and went. Didn't even question it.

You see, God had been speaking to my heart about the Havasupai ... about actually moving down to the canyon ... but I had been putting Him off and making excuses. I told God that I was praying for revival in America and I hadn't finished that yet. He told me He was taking care of that and to look around. All across the nation were signs that said, "Pray for America." Even casinos and beer joints had such signs — their owners apparently not realizing that if God really showed up in power, they would likely be shut down.

So I said yes to God on two conditions: 1) my wife Denise had to be in agreement, and 2) she and I would be accepted into the U.S. Missions program with the Assemblies of God. This was not a problem for God. My wife agreed and we were accepted into the missions program for orientation the following March even though we had applied way beyond the cutoff date. We raised our budget in nine months and were ready to go to Supai the following year.

I lived in a tent down in Supai off and on for six weeks. Then some men came down and helped me build an 8'x12' bunkhouse. I lived in that bunkhouse for six months while I built a 450-square foot house for my family out behind the home of Loren and his wife Janice. We also had a small trailer in Kingman, Arizona, to use whenever we needed to take a break and buy more supplies.

My family spent two years living down in the canyon, learning about the people. It was quite a change in culture going from our home in Tennessee to living in the bottom of the Grand Canyon on a reservation. We had many outreaches and helped people the best we could. I learned a lot about the hardships of Native people. Loren and Janice treated us like family. They were awesome.

I feel it best not to disclose too much about the lives of the Supai people in this book. I must also let you know about some things I did wrong.

When you enter a reservation, you are entering the land of a sovereign nation. I had permission from Loren and Janice to stay, but not from the Havasupai tribal council. The only outsiders that had received permission to live there were school teachers and some Wycliffe Bible translators. Some of the council liked us, but some didn't. It became a point of contention and a hardship on our hosts, so we made the decision to leave.

I was a little upset at having sown a couple years of my family's life down in the canyon without seeing the fruit that I had wanted to see. It felt like failure. I had tried every way I could to build a church in the village only to see Mormons come in and build across the way. In my experience, they treated the Supai as second class citizens, which is not what Jesus would do.

I took our furniture, tents, tools, and supplies, and left town. Looking back, I should have left most of my stuff for the people of Supai.

My family would spend the next three years on top of the canyon near the Hualapai Reservation in Truxton, Arizona. We had ten acres of land and worked at building a church and high school for some of the kids of Supai because at the time, only about ten percent would graduate from high school, the rest being sent to boarding schools after eighth grade. I traveled, preached, raised money, and worked on getting teams to come and help us build. Many did come and help.

During this time, however, I suffered heart trouble and wound up in an emergency room … twice. A pacemaker was inserted and for the next three years, I would struggle with medication that produced a lot of unpleasant side effects including insomnia, high cholesterol, anxiety, panic attacks, and diabetes.

Having received permission from the Assemblies of God church district to sell the property, I shut down the work in Truxton and moved the family back to Tennessee where Denise could be with her mother who, we would come to find out, was battling cancer. She would eventually lose that battle.

We incurred a lot of credit card debt due to my medical bills and some other things. My physical condition allowed me only about four good hours per day. However, God provided me with a young man named James who began traveling with me and helping in the ministry. I would preach, rest most of the day, then preach again. It was about all I had energy for. But I refused to give up.

Now, what can I say from all of this? Well, I learned a lot about Native culture. The Supai experience opened the door for me to go and preach on many more reservations. It opened the door to a great relationship with many Native ministries. I have been blessed to preach revivals and labor among Native American people including the Makah, Blackfeet, Ute, Havasupai, Hualapai, Hopi, Apache, Navajo, Pascua Yaqui, Mohave, Salt River, Lumbee, Coushatta, Chitimacha, Alabama-Coushatta, Choctaw, Chickasaw, Cherokee, and others. I tell you this so you will know that what may look like failure in your eyes may not at all look like failure in God's eyes.

I have also been blessed to preach in many villages in Alaska. In some instances, James and I had to take a small plane, even snowmobiles, to reach certain villages. God always gave me enough energy to keep going. And everywhere I went, people prayed for my heart. It was amazing. I saw people get healed from all sorts of things even though I wasn't getting healed.

Then, near the end of an eight-week tour that took me from Tennessee through Arkansas and on to New Mexico, Mexico, and Alaska, it happened. James and I were in Delta Junction, Alaska, preaching at Living Waters Assembly of God. It was Saturday, October 30, 2010. God said to me, "Stop taking the medicine." So I did. For the next four days, my body went through withdrawals. I stayed in bed and rested most of the time. The following Friday, James and I flew from Fairbanks to Point Hope on the Chukchi Sea in northwestern Alaska and started revival that weekend. I never took another heart pill.

I visited my heart doctor a year later. After testing me for proof, all he could do was shake his head, wave his hands, and walk out of the room. Praise God! And not only that, but by year end, almost all of my credit card debt would be canceled.

Never give up. The journey into the apostolic is not an easy one, but you must never quit!

11

Revelation

December 2005. Stanford, Kentucky. It was a Thursday night. I was scheduled to conduct a one-night revival service with Pastor Shane. We had met a couple weeks earlier in Hodgenville at the church of my friend, Pastor Mike Williams, where Shane had been preaching an extended revival. I had filled in for him a couple days when he had to be somewhere else, and returned the following week to hear him preach. I preached at a few churches in the Louisville area before it came time to do the service in Stanford. Don Carver, an evangelist friend of mine, scheduled the Kentucky meetings.

Pastor Mike, a prophet of God, had told Shane, "You need to have Bill at your church. The same thing that is happening here is going to break out over there." I didn't put a lot of stock in that prophesy. But God apparently did, as I would soon come to find out.

With me was a young man named Jonathan Landis who I had been mentoring for the past year. We first met when the

Brownsville Revival School of Ministry sent a mission team to Supai while I was there. After graduating from the school in December, he came to Supai to work with me in January. In September, he and I went out on the road for about eight weeks, raising missions support and preaching revivals. He would become engaged to my daughter Tara before the year was up. My youngest daughter Rhiannon joined us for the last two weeks of the trip. The three of us traveled in a one-ton truck with a travel trailer.

Pulling into a campground in Danville, about eleven miles up the road from Stanford, I said to the Lord, "I'm tired. I've been on the road for a while. We've had some chances for revival, but I'm ready to get this over with and drive back home to Tennessee and sleep in my own bed tonight and have some home-cooked meals." We unhooked the trailer, got ourselves ready for the service, and headed out for Stanford. On the way down, I had another talk with the Lord. I said, "Lord, forgive me. If You want to do something tonight, You go ahead and do it. I'm not in a hurry to get home. I don't have to be home, but I want to do what You want to do."

The church building where the service was to be held looked almost like a Cracker Barrel Old Country Store and Restaurant. We parked the truck, went inside, and soon found ourselves in an open room used for the church sanctuary. At the very back of this room was a prayer room. We walked back to it, opened the door, and entered in.

Man, it just looked like heaven in there. Hanging from the ceiling of the ten by fourteen-foot room was a luxurious-looking, rather clear material having a bit of gold shade to it with little white Christmas lights scattered throughout. The floor was covered in a nice, thick carpet. There was some antique furniture in there. I'm telling you, the atmosphere of heaven was in that place. And not only the atmosphere of heaven, but the very presence of it … pervading the entire room!

I sat myself down on a couch and began to pray. As I did, I could feel the presence of God coming upon me. The glory of God began to permeate my body. I could feel that heaviness, that weightiness of His glory. It got heavier … and heavier … and heavier until—as I recall—I just slid off of the couch and melted onto the floor. Besides Jonathan and Rhiannon, Pastor Shane and a few others were also in there praying.

God poured His Spirit into me as I laid on the carpet wondering, *What is God gonna do tonight?* I could hardly move my body. It felt like I was almost paralyzed. I then heard somebody tell us it was time for the service to start. I'm thinking, *Service to start? I can hardly get up off of the floor.*

Some tried to sort of ease out of there and crawl into the sanctuary. If I remember correctly, the congregation had already begun doing praise and worship. I somehow managed to get myself up before stumbling and crawling my way out into the sanctuary. I said to myself, "Something is going to happen in this place tonight."

We could hardly get through the worship. I stood up and tried to minister for maybe ten or twelve minutes, but the presence of God was so strong. People were falling out of their chairs. Rhiannon couldn't even get through the worship as she was down on her face before the Lord. We resorted to simply praying for each other as people were laid out all over the sanctuary. Chairs were moved out of the way as people fell down and rolled around.

My body felt as though it was covered with a blanket of hot oil. I was tingling all over. I could have laid on the floor for hours. The peace of God was upon everyone. I don't think anyone was left standing. There was such a weightiness in that place. It was the glory of the Lord. It felt very much like it did when I attended the Brownsville Revival.

Jonathan, Rhiannon, and I were eventually able to get up off the floor and return to the campground in Danville. But the tingling sensation continued to stay with me. Whenever I slowed down or laid down, I would feel that heavy glory hit me again. It was awesome.

I had talked with Pastor Shane about the service and we decided to meet for another night to see what God would do. There went my plans for going home. We then decided to extend services through Saturday and Sunday as well to see what all might happen.

In getting touched that Thursday night, I became drunk in the Spirit and would remain that way for the next seven days. I was overflowing night and day. On Friday night, the Spirit was on me even more than Thursday night. By Saturday morning, I could hardly sleep. Between Friday night and early Saturday morning, I maybe slept a total of two hours. It felt as though high voltage electricity was running through my body. I would sleep a little bit, then wake up and tremble, not out of fear, but simply because there was such a strong presence of the Lord flowing throughout my body that I couldn't really do much else, let alone sleep. I felt like I was going to blow up. Sometimes I would pray, "Lord, back it off a little bit or I'm going to die." Then I'd say, "No, Lord. I want all I can get."

I got to thinking that what I needed to do was find a way to release some of the power. So that Saturday morning, I began calling people from my cell phone. Now, when I call people around six or seven o'clock in the morning, they think something must be wrong because I usually sleep in after having been up so late. So, if I'm calling that early, they know something's up.

I wound up calling about fifteen or sixteen people. A person would answer, "Hello, who is this?" and all I could do was laugh. The joy of the Lord was bubbling out of my spirit over the phone and onto the person at the other end. Many became affected by the Spirit as I laughed. I might hear the person on the other end of the line begin to laugh, then drop the phone and fall to the floor. Some would begin to cry. I had to release what God was filling me up with. And almost everyone I called said they really needed it. They got touched.

Imagine the power of God flowing through your telephone and touching someone on the other end. The Holy Spirit works in mysterious ways sometimes. But so what. It's time to get Him out of the box.

I was still in pretty bad shape that Saturday ... in a manner of speaking. I could hardly get out of bed or walk around or do much of anything. I was just so drunk in the Holy Spirit. Eventually, I was able to eat some lunch and get ready for the service that night. But it would be the same scene on Sunday. I would just continue on as the Spirit of God kept flowing.

The power of the Holy Spirit was moving in a mighty way. Everybody coming into the church building was getting touched. People were staying late. Some crawled out of the building, trying to get home. Others had to have someone drive them home.

Now, you might be thinking, *What is this? Why would God do this?* I'll tell you why. It's because God was refreshing the body of Christ, giving encouragement and strength to His church. Some people received emotional healing. Some received physical healing. Some were just dry, wandering through a desert, and God let streams of living water flow into their desert, bringing joy into their lives. The Bible says that when Philip preached revival in the city of Samaria, great joy came to that city (see Acts 8:5, 8).

On Sunday evening, the Lord spoke to me and said that I was to fast on Monday, Tuesday, and Wednesday, and that I wasn't even supposed to go to church or preach those nights. Pastor Shane and I had decided to extend revival but, *I'm not even supposed to go preach those nights? Oh man!* I had to call Shane and tell him I was not coming to church on Monday, Tuesday, or Wednesday because the Lord wanted me to just fast and pray and seek His face. And that's what I began to do. So Pastor Shane filled in for me on those nights.

Ever since the previous Thursday night, I had been

flowing continually in the presence of God. I was weak. It was hard to walk or do anything. It's a good thing I didn't have to go to a job because I was just too drunk. Drunk in the Holy Spirit.

On Wednesday morning, seven days later, as I tried to get out of bed and move around, all of a sudden the Lord began downloading stuff to me, most of it having to do with the office of Apostle and the five-fold ministry. He showed me Acts 3:20-21 where it speaks about Jesus not returning to earth "until the period of restoration of all things." While this scripture may mean other things, God was showing me the restoration of the five-fold ministry; that Jesus is not coming back until the five-fold ministry is fulfilled.

"He gave some as apostles, and some as prophets, and some as evangelists, and some as pastors and teachers, for the equipping of the saints for the work of [the ministry], to the building up of the body of Christ" (Ephesians 4:11-12).

We began to see the beginning of the restoration of the prophet in the late 80s and early 90s. The prophet then began prophesying that the apostles were coming. Beginning in the 90s, we started to see the rise of the apostle. And why is that?

Well, we keep praying and asking God to pour out revival like it's described in the Book of Acts, but in order for that presence and power of the Holy Spirit to come and move in such a way that the blind will see, the lame will walk, and the dead will be raised to life, there has to be a wineskin ... a covering ... a government—something to keep it all going in God's direction. We need an apostolic covering. An apostolic relationship.

We need apostles who will not compromise the Word of God. Men of God who will not compromise truth but go after God. Men who can't be bought or sold and won't be worried about anything. They will be humble men *and* women of God so that when God pours out His power in tremendous ways and revival happens, they will know how to steward it.

In times past, we didn't know how to steward revival or

keep it going. We saw flashes of revival. We maybe saw a couple of years of revival. But until we have God's government in place, I don't believe we will see continual revival.

To see the fullness of the kingdom come and the saints equipped for the work of the ministry, we must have the five-fold ministry operating in our churches; not just pastors here and evangelists there, but teams of people working in churches to release the gifts of God through those churches.

1 Corinthians 12:28 says, "And God has appointed in the church, first apostles, second prophets, third teachers, then miracles, then gifts of healings, helps, administrations, various kinds of tongues." You see? God appointed this thing! The scripture doesn't say that an apostle, prophet, teacher, or any other person with a particular gifting for the church is to be voted on by man.

We must create an environment in which the five-fold ministry can evolve. God is the one who does the calling while the Church body is to recognize and affirm the spiritual gifts He gives. When the five-fold ministry is allowed to function as it should, the Saints will be equipped to take over the world.

Another thing God showed me was the river flowing from His throne room. In Ezekiel 47 we read of the prophet who, in a vision, was led by a man out a thousand cubits into waters that were ankle-deep, then another thousand cubits into waters that were knee-deep, then another thousand cubits into waters that were waist-deep, and yet another thousand cubits to "enough water to swim in." God was giving me a revelation on that scripture.

What He was showing me is that the ankle-deep water is like a pastor or teacher anointing. It's in the river of life. It's where people are born again. It's ministering to those people. It's building a foundation. It's only ankle-deep, so it's not hard to stand there. It's very stable. It's nurturing. It's encouraging. It's bringing people along. It's discipling.

Then there's the next level where the water is knee-deep. This is where we see the evangelist. It's a little harder to stand here because the deeper the water, the more it's like a river. There are miracles happening—healings and deliverance that lead to a great harvest of souls coming into the kingdom. Yet, it's still easy to stand in these waters because it's only knee-deep. I think of Philip the evangelist in Acts, chapter 8, where we read of miracles happening, causing many people to believe in Jesus and be baptized in water. However, it wouldn't be until the apostles came and laid hands on them that they would receive an impartation of the Holy Ghost.

The next level out is waist-deep. Here we have the prophet. The prophet is *out there*. He's moving in the miraculous, the signs and wonders. He's prophesying what's coming. If you're in waist-deep running water, it can be pretty hard to stand up. It's kind of shaky and—if you can receive this—it's an increase in the supernatural coming into the Church, the body of Christ. And so, the prophet is out there and the water's running. His feet are still on the ground. That's important. His feet are on the ground, but the water's pushing him and he's just about to lose it. He almost feels out of control. He's pretty radical. His feet being on the ground represents ministry happening in the Church.

The move of God is happening in the Church. The move could be a pastor-teacher revival where people are being discipled and cared for. It could be an evangelistic revival where people are coming into the kingdom of God. It could be a prophetic revival where people are being prophesied over and receiving personal ministry. However, the entire ministry is happening in the Church. Now, most of the time the congregation is told to go out and get people and bring them into the church so that they may be touched by the gifts flowing through the man or woman of God, when what should be happening is the man or woman of God should be equipping the church to do the work of ministry outside the four walls.

We now come to the place of the apostolic. Here, you're swimming because the waters are deep. And the river's flowing. The apostolic anointing is like that running river. As an apostle, you're really not in control of anything; you just flow wherever the river takes you. And this is where things really happen—the exceedingly abundant supernatural, above and beyond anything anyone could believe or ask for. This is the level that the first apostles operated in.

In the Book of Acts, the third chapter, we read of Peter and John coming upon a man lame from birth who would sit each day at the Beautiful Gate of the temple begging for alms. In the name of Jesus, Peter commanded him to rise up and walk. He then took the man by his right hand and lifted him up, whereupon the man leaped and walked with the two apostles to the temple, praising God.

In the fifth chapter, we find men and women bringing their sick out into the streets "so that when Peter came by at least his shadow might fall on any one of them," and a multitude from surrounding cities bringing the sick and tormented, all of them getting healed.

In the ninth chapter, we read of a woman named Tabitha who became ill and died. As Peter happened to be in a nearby town, disciples quickly sent for him. Arriving at the woman's home, Peter had the mourners leave the room where she lay. He then knelt down, prayed, turned to the body, and said, "Tabitha, arise." The woman opened her eyes and sat up … alive … raised from the dead.

In those days, powerful, miraculous things were happening. In these days, the same sort of things will begin to happen when we create a wineskin for the apostolic. When all five offices work together, it increases the effectiveness of all.

At the apostolic level, you get in a flow of where you're not in control; of where you're no longer "pressing in" to try and make things happen. You're not pressing against the heavens to try to get a breakthrough because heaven has broken through to you and you're just flowing with the Spirit. There's no effort to it at all. You just touch people, pray for people, speak the Word, and things happen. It's like Jesus' effortless ministry. You go wherever the Spirit goes. Where the river goes, that's where you go, and it brings life.

There have been apostolic revivals. At the beginning of this book, I mentioned the Brownsville Revival. During the times I visited that revival, I didn't understand what was happening. I couldn't figure out what was different about that revival from revivals of the past. God was now revealing to me what had taken place at the Brownsville Revival. The reason people could come in, get saved, prayed for, and then immediately go out and begin to Do The Stuff was because there was an apostolic anointing in the house—Brownsville Assembly of God. I believe Pastor John Kilpatrick was an apostle over that house. And while some folks had a difficult time understanding his ministry, there wasn't a wineskin for him to fill in the office of Apostle, to be a father over other houses. In fact, following his resignation from Brownsville, I read a statement in *The Remnant* (a revival newspaper) in which he was quoted as saying to his congregation, "The one thing I wish I had done was taught you more about the office of an apostle."

I had seen people at Brownsville get saved, pray 'the sinner's prayer,' and then be invited for special prayer to receive "more of the Lord." Prayer teams would come down from the platform, lay hands on people, and release an impartation into those people for more of the Lord. The fruit of it was that those who received the impartation would go out and Do The Stuff. It was an apostolic impartation and I don't think anybody realized it. It didn't have to be prayer from one of the leaders of the revival because the prayer team members were flowing in that apostolic atmosphere. Receiving the impartation or anointing didn't mean those people were now apostles; yet they could begin to walk in apostolic power. It wasn't about *what* they knew, but *Who* they knew.

The same Spirit that had been working in the sanctuary was now taking it to the streets. No longer would the testimony be, "I got saved back at that revival" or, "Somebody prophesied over my life" or, "I got healed back there." It was now a live demonstration of Holy Ghost power. It wasn't about *telling* a testimony, but *demonstrating* a testimony. "What God did for me, He's now going to do for you. I'm going to lay hands on you and the power of God is going to come upon you. God is going to baptize you in the Holy Spirit. God is going to heal your body. God is going to save you. You're about to have an encounter with the living God."

In previous revivals, the Lord would speak and the power of God would move in the Church. He moved in power through those operating in pastoral, teaching, evangelistic, and prophetic ministries. People got touched and were healed, delivered and set free. But when those people left the building, their testimony to others was that the same thing could happen to them if they would come to their church. They would go down the road and invite people to come to their church and receive their miracle from the great man or woman of God. That was then.

We are now in the day of restoration of the five-fold ministry and God is taking it up a notch. No longer is the miraculous going to be about the great man or woman of God. It's going to be about a nameless, faceless generation that preaches the gospel and demonstrates it with signs, wonders and miracles following. In apostolic revival, when people get touched, healed and delivered, they head out of the building not to *tell* about God's power, but to *demonstrate* it. "God's called *me* to lay hands on you." "God's called *me* to pray for the sick." This is what God is about to do on the earth.

It's going to take an apostolic anointing and impartation with God equipping the saints—every one of them—to do the work of ministry; not to go knock on doors and hand out tracts, but to demonstrate the power of Jesus. We will call things that are not ... into being as though they were. We will call men and women that God is raising up to be apostles as though they already were.

I believe one trait that apostles have is a burning desire to see their gifts imparted to the body of Christ. A shortcoming of the great healing revivals of the 50s was that there were only a limited number of people flowing in gifts of healings. What if they had been able to multiply themselves in the body of Christ? What would have happened if say, there had been five thousand A.A. Allens? Or five thousand William Branhams? Or five thousand Oral Robertses? There may not have been a sick person in all of America.

Many in the Church have such a hard time when someone says "apostle" or "prophet." They rise up and proclaim that there can't be any apostles or prophets, yet they don't have a problem with pastor, evangelist, and teacher which are not only in the same book (Ephesians), the same chapter (4), and the very same verse (11), but occurring *after* apostle and prophet. They're all right there, right next to each other. So why would we discard the first two but keep the last three?

I believe as we speak out, "Yes, that man of God and that woman of God *are* prophets! Yes, that man of God and woman of God *are* apostles!" we will be empowering those called by God to flow in their calling. At the same time, we will be enabling ourselves to come under the anointing that God wants us to flow in.

As I said earlier in this book, I believe a trait of an apostle is to be a jack of all trades and a master of none; in other words, a person who can flow in the prophetic, the evangelistic, the pastoral, and the teaching without any one being the apostle's life calling. In fact, after a while an apostle will realize that none of the four offices is 'home.' I believe apostles must spend time walking in each office before they can truly walk in the apostolic.

Up until that Wednesday morning in December, it never seemed like I really fit into one place of ministry. "Here's Brother Bill the missionary." Well, I did that for a couple of years, but it just didn't feel right. "Here's Brother Bill the evangelist." Yes, I've done that, but it's not my life calling. "Here's Brother Bill the pastor." Done that too, but that isn't my life calling either. But now God was beginning to show me what an apostle is. He began to show me that this is what I am. And it fit.

We make a mistake when our calling becomes our identity. Our identity should be as Sons and Daughters of God. Our calling is simply how we function in the body of Christ; it's what we do.

Prior to this day, it felt like nothing fit. But the office of Apostle, that fit. It didn't make me greater than anyone else. The call of Apostle is a calling that God has given to the Church and we need to stop being ashamed of it. We need to stop being afraid to say the word *apostle* or to speak over those who God has called to be apostles.

Generally, those called by God to be apostles don't want to go around announcing it to everyone. But as we recognize this calling on their lives and affirm it, we will allow them to flow in the ministry that God wants them to flow in.

I believe it's a ministry of impartation and that soon we will be seeing more and more apostolic men and women laying hands on other people and releasing an impartation, then sending them out to do the same. Paul told Timothy to stir up the gift of God that was in him through the laying on of his [Paul's] hands (see 2 Timothy 1:6).

This must be taught. And it must be caught. I am not saying this is the only way, for some simply spend time in their prayer closets, are anointed by the Holy Spirit, then go out and Do The Stuff. I nonetheless believe God wants to use teaching and impartation of Apostles and Prophets to equip the masses to Do The Stuff.

The apostolic authority is like that of a sheriff. In Hardin County, Tennessee, where I reside, we have a sheriff. He's over the county. We also have deputy sheriffs. Not one of them is Sheriff, but Deputy Sheriff; yet each walks under the same authority as Sheriff. They're all out there, in the county, and should anyone of them have reason to stop at your house and serve you a warrant, it's no different than if the sheriff himself showed up on your doorstep. If you incur a traffic violation and any one of them pulls you over, his car and badge may say "Deputy Sheriff," but the authority he carries is the same as that of "Sheriff."

Just as there is a natural authority, there is a spiritual authority. As we come under and build relationship with those who are apostles and prophets, we will flow in the same anointing they do. We will be walking in apostolic authority under the covering, safety, and protection they walk in because we have given them access in our lives as fathers in the faith. This is not a power struggle; it's family. We will keep the word of God in our heart. We will not sell out to religious politicians and church administrators who would compromise the anointing and try to run the church like a corporation.

Apostles will catch a lot of flak and undergo a lot of persecution because they won't be satisfied with church status quo. They won't be satisfied with just getting along and trying to make everyone happy. They will go after heaven and only be satisfied when they see heaven invade earth. They won't be satisfied unless people's lives are being radically changed and they see those people raised up and sent out to do the work of the ministry. They won't be satisfied until the sick are being healed, the lame are walking, the deaf are hearing, and the blind are seeing. They won't be satisfied until this gospel is preached throughout the entire world.

We've had far more than enough people in religious circles and denominations satisfied with the status quo. They didn't like apostles because they were thorns in the flesh, not wanting to build big buildings or big bank accounts or store up a lot of money, but to take the gospel around the world. So they either kicked them out or waited for them to die out so they could do church their way.

Enter the politicians and administrators. The administrator can keep the checkbook and grow the money, putting it in savings accounts to accumulate interest, ensuring that the corporation keeps running. The politician meanwhile can smooth things over with the big givers, compromising the word of God as he sees fit. After about a hundred years of this, we see most denominations declining in numbers and Spiritual power.

I happen to believe that most denominations were founded by apostolic movements, but somewhere along the way the apostle was either kicked out or died out. The congregation said, "No, we really don't want him anymore because he keeps pushing us to go to other nations. He keeps pushing us to go out. He makes us uncomfortable. We've got our dynasty built here. We have our health club. We have our gymnasium. We have our community. Everybody is happy. But the apostle keeps pushing us, telling us we need to go out and preach the gospel."

I also happen to believe that God is in the process of bringing down the politicians. He's bringing down the administrators in our denominations. Churches that have gone a hundred years or so are dying out because they lost their vision to take the gospel around the world, focusing instead on building empires.

Those called to be apostles will not be satisfied apart from training, equipping, raising up, and reaching the world with the gospel of Jesus Christ. I believe this is the last push, as it were, as we see apostles being raised up. We will see the power of God operating through the office of Apostle as it did in the early days of the church of Acts.

As God gave me all this revelation, I wrote it down. I had

about seventeen pages of notes on the Apostle given to me by the Lord on Wednesday morning. That night, I went to church and preached.

Afterwards, I shared with Brother Shane what was going on and what God had revealed to me. Since he had scheduled a prophetic conference in London, Tennessee, we shut down revival to attend that conference. Denise and Tara drove up to meet us in London that Friday.

The Church of God hosting the conference was a real blessing to us. We were provided a house to stay in as soon as we arrived. I quickly took advantage of that to settle down a bit. However, while waiting in my bedroom for Denise to show up, the Spirit of the Lord suddenly came upon me. I began to weep ... and travail ... and intercede ... with groanings and utterances I couldn't really understand.

The presence of the Spirit kept coming over me. The weeping and travailing went on for a good couple of hours. I couldn't stop. It was as if I was giving birth to something. My stomach became tight and sore from all the weeping.

Eventually, I was able to regain some control before Denise and Tara arrived. We went out for dinner, then returned to the house, got ready for the service, and went over to the church. As we joined in prayer with a number of people prior to the service, it hit me again: weeping ... travailing ... interceding. Others began praying for me as it seemed God was birthing something in me. That something, I came to believe, was an apostolic ministry.

That night, even though other speakers had been ministering and I wasn't scheduled to speak, Brother Shane asked me, "Do you want to release what God's given you?" I had been pacing back and forth across the back of the church. I guess people might have thought I was crazy. But something was burning like a fire inside of me and was about to explode. So I said, "Yes."

I got up in front of the church and said to those gathered,

"Well, this is going to be history or heresy, one or the other, but I believe this is what God's releasing tonight." I then began to share what I was learning about the apostolic ministry. The people were open to what I was saying. In fact, God had already been speaking to a lot of them about it. So I asked, "Who wants this anointing? I believe there is going to be an apostolic impartation tonight."

Many people came forward. Many who had already received prayer came up again. There was a long line of people wanting prayer. I went down through the line and laid my hands on them, praying for the anointing to be released for them to go and do the works of Jesus. God had given me a message to carry and many people got touched that night.

The following weekend, I went to see Pastor Mike in Hodgenville and shared the message with him. After Christmas, I returned to Pastor Shane's church where we started revival that lasted upwards of four or five weeks. God also began opening doors for me to continue traveling and speaking to people.

I went down to The Ramp in Hamilton, Alabama, where Sister Karen Wheaton allowed me to share a bit and pray for people there one night. Later that night, two couples approached me to say they didn't know what office God had called them to because most people don't recognize the office of Apostle, but that they felt my message had affirmed their calling.

I shared my message with a few pastors here and there. I discussed the message with friends and asked them what they thought about it from a doctrinal standpoint. The denomination I was in at the time didn't believe that apostles and prophets were for today even though it's known as a "Pentecostal" denomination, believing in the gifts of tongues and other spiritual gifts, and of course, pastors, evangelists and teachers.

Regardless, God spoke to me and showed me that apostles and prophets *are* for today. This is not a different scripture. It really isn't. Again, it's all right there in the same verse: "He gave some as apostles, and some as prophets, and some as evangelists, and some as pastors and teachers, for the equipping of the saints for the work of [the ministry], to the building up of the body of Christ" (Ephesians 4:11–12).

It had been about eight years from the time God spoke a word to me through J. Konrad Hölé in Tennessee. Remember, he had said, "God's called you to be an apostle." Eight years from the time I attended the Brownsville Revival to traveling on the road to praying for America and asking, "God, what's your calling on my life? What do you have for me to do?" And it was on a Wednesday morning in December, after seven days of being drunk in the Spirit, when God said, "This is your calling."

Finally, I felt comfortable knowing that God had called me to be an apostle. I wasn't comfortable in telling people that, but I knew it was what God had called me to do.

There are many of you out there who don't fit into any one slot or calling because you weren't made to fit into one. You weren't made to fit into the pastor slot, the evangelist slot, the teaching slot, or even the prophetic slot because God has called you to be an apostle. We need to recognize and affirm one another in the apostolic calling. It doesn't mean you get a bigger, newer car to drive in and that people will open doors for you and roll out the red carpet for you. If anything, it probably means you will go to places you've never been to before—if even heard of—and that life will get a little tougher instead of a little easier. Your finances may even drop a bit, particularly if you're already in the ministry, as many people will not understand what you're doing. But it's time. The time has come for the restoration of all things. And that restoration is not coming until people who are called to be apostles fulfill the role that God has called them to walk in.

Others prophesied of my apostolic calling and God later affirmed it. I believe God wants to prophesy your calling into your life. Many of you out there are searching and wondering. I pray this book will speak to your life about what God is calling you to do, in the mighty name of Jesus. Hallelujah. Amen.

12

Manifestation

Early in 2010 I began receiving email. It's not unusual for me to receive email. But this email was from India. A young man—I presumed he was young—wrote to me saying, "Pastor Bill. We love you very much. We have been watching your YouTube videos on the Internet and we see the power of God moving and we need you very much. Please come to India. Come and pray for us. Come pray for the anointing. Come pray for the fire of God to fall in India, to fall on us."

I had no idea who was sending the email. I didn't know if it was just somebody getting on the Internet and wanting money, or what. These days, you just don't have a clue sometimes. I wondered if it might be someone secretly wanting to destroy me; to get me to India ten thousand miles away and just take me out into the woods and beat me up or something. So I didn't think much about it. But the emails kept coming, about one or two per month, saying, "Please come to India. Please pray for us. We love you." I would reply, "We love you too. We're praying for you.

God bless you. Have a great day."

After about a year of receiving the emails, I decided to contact James, the young man who had been traveling with me. He and I had ministered in Mexico, Alaska, and all over America. I asked him, "What do you think about going to India?" He got excited about that. We had passports. So all we needed were visas, which wouldn't be too hard to get. He said, "Okay, I'll go." So we determined to go.

Our plan was to fly to India, and if no one was waiting at the airport to meet us, we would wait a few days and then fly back. We were trusting God that the people on the other end were who they said they were and that He would move in the situation.

In early 2011, I resigned from Assemblies of God U.S. Missions to start my own ministry: Global Apostolic Revival Network (GARN). I had felt a shift coming when my daughter Rhiannon and I took a five-thousand mile journey the previous July. The two of us ministered in Arkansas, Arizona, Mexico, Montana, Colorado, and Missouri. I was raising money to live in Alaska and start a ministry on the North Slope, but God seemed to put a stop to that. I got the impression He didn't want me to settle in anywhere on a permanent basis, but to be flexible and ready to go wherever He might lead me.

I had tried to fit into the mold cast for "normal" ministry, but it just didn't work. U.S. Missions didn't really have a job title for what I was doing in the U.S. And now I was headed overseas.

James and I didn't have a clue as to where God might be leading us. *What is it like in India? What do they eat? Where do they shop? What is their transportation?* We knew nothing. Fortunately, prior to making travel arrangements, I was able to connect via cell phone with the young man who had been emailing me. His name is Jashuva (like a form of Joshua). He spoke in a broken English he had learned primarily by way of comparing biblical scriptures written in Telugu (his native language) with those written in English. He was very excited and happy to be able to visit with me over the phone. As I prayed with him, the power of the Holy Spirit began to touch him even though he was ten thousand miles away. I told him, "We're coming to India." We scheduled the visit for April. Jashuva said, "It's going to be warm that time of the year, but it'll work out."

That April, James and I set out on our journey to India that would involve three flights. We arrived at Nashville International Airport in plenty of time. However, bad weather in Chicago caused our first leg to be cancelled. We went to a ticket counter to try and catch a second flight, but it too had been cancelled. We eventually managed to get booked on a third flight but had little time to catch it, so we took off running for the end of the terminal, tickets and bags in hand. I had told James beforehand, "We are not checking our bags. We are taking only what we can carry in our hands because when we get there [to India] we can't wait for our bags to come in. We need to be ready to go." We reached the end of the terminal just in time — to see our plane pull away. We now had to go all the way out and through Security again to get back to the ticket counter.

Stepping up to the counter, I asked the agent about the possibility of getting on another flight. She said, "Well, I'm sorry. There are no more flights today. You will just have to wait until tomorrow. We'll try to get you a hotel."

I said, "Man, there's got to be a flight today." I got out my iPhone, pulled up Orbitz, and guess what? There was a flight leaving Nashville that day with a connection to India. I held my phone up to the agent and said, "Look here, right on my phone. There's a flight leaving soon." She took a look ... and got us booked ... on Lufthansa — an *outstanding* airline. Instead of having to go through Chicago, we would now be flying to Atlanta; then to Frankfurt, Germany; and from there to Hyderabad, India.

Neither James nor I had ever taken such a long flight. Man, do you know how far ten thousand miles is in an airplane? It's a long ways!

We landed in Hyderabad around 11:00 PM ... the following day. We were a bit jet-lagged, but doing alright. Passing through Customs, we emerged into an area where we found a crowd of people waiting for arriving passengers. There, waiting for us, was Jashuva and his dad, Pastor Daniel. They were as excited to see us as we were them. It was like family connecting, like long lost family members reuniting.

Since neither Jashuva or Daniel drove — let alone owned — a motor vehicle, they had to travel to the airport by train, car, bus and taxi, which meant we had to remain at the airport for eight hours until we could catch the next train back to their village. Praise God, there was a McDonald's in that airport, even if chicken was the only meat on the menu.

Early the next morning, the four of us hopped on a bus for a one-hour ride across town before taking a little taxi the rest of the way to the train station. Fatigue was beginning to set in. After waiting three hours at the train station, we all boarded a train to ride the rails ... for seven hours. James and I were looking forward to getting a good night's sleep as soon as we could get it.

After the lengthy train ride, we had to travel three more hours by car to Palakollu in the state of Andhra Pradesh in southeastern India. There, we pulled into a hospital where Pastor Daniel's daughter had given birth to a boy only a couple days earlier. Praise the Lord, having had the opportunity to pray for her over the phone prior to leaving America, I now had the opportunity to see her and pray for her in person.

We then went to a hotel. There, James and I laid down our bags. I said to Pastor Daniel, "Please give us a day to sleep and rest after two and a half days of traveling before we preach." We laid down on our beds. Hard beds. Apparently, there had been some miscommunication along the way because Pastor Daniel replied, "Pastor, we must go out right now and preach the gospel. We must go preach the gospel!" I said, "Okay."

Having rented a car and driver for the week, the four of us

got in the car and were taken out of town. I had no idea where we were going. There were no road signs along the way, yet villages everywhere ... villages and people ... lots of people.

Everywhere James and I looked there were people. I had noticed that from the time we left the airport in Hyderabad, neither of us had seen another white person ... or African-American ... or Hispanic ... Only Indian people. Lots and lots of Indian people.

We eventually arrived in a village where a little church was hosting an open air meeting. There was music playing. They had set up some lights and sound equipment for which I had previously sent down funds to help rent. There were maybe eighty to a hundred people in attendance.

Now, getting to Hyderabad had been one thing for James and me, but between the added waits and travel by bus, taxi, and train to Palakollu, well, it just did us in. Not to mention the little trip from town to where we were now ... wherever that was. We were exhausted. What better time to see whether the same gospel and the same Holy Spirit we had been preaching in America would work in India on the other side of the world.

A number of people had commented on my YouTube videos with statements such as, "You are hypnotizing people. When people fall down and shake and get healed, it's just the power of suggestion that the Holy Spirit will come on them. It's all just manipulation and it's not real." Well, James and I were about to put that to the test. For here we were, in some little village in a far-away land where nobody really knew us and our hosts couldn't even translate for us very well.

No one really knew what to expect. After laying hands on six people who felt something as they were touched by the presence of God, and then laying hands on a seventh and seeing him fall to the floor under the power of God, everyone knew there was no manipulation involved. When we laid our hands on the sick and the power of the Holy Spirit came upon them and healed their bodies right then and there, no one questioned whether the power of God was real. It was, and is, real. Very real. We have this confidence in God that what He promises, He will do. And He was doing it.

Jashuva told us that they had never seen people 'fall out' in the Holy Spirit. There was no power of suggestion, no pushing of people to the ground; just the power of God moving among them. I believe God was releasing apostolic power into that village.

One lady was so sick she could hardly stand up. She was pregnant and in very bad condition. She couldn't even repeat a prayer with me. But only a few minutes after I prayed for her, she was totally healed, walking around and rejoicing in the Lord. Hallelujah. Praise God!

I'm convinced that the same Holy Spirit moving in America is the same Holy Spirit that wants to go around the entire world and see the gospel preached. When God sends you out thousands of miles from home, He wants to demonstrate His power and presence with signs, wonders and miracles following you.

This was only the beginning of the trip for James and me. Over the next couple of days, we would visit with another man of God: Pastor Easu. We preached to pastors in his network and ministered at an orphanage under his care.

We also visited his father's open air church in a nearby village. As we began to preach at that meeting, the electricity went out. But that didn't stop us. We turned on a couple flashlights, held them up, and preached that Jesus is the light of the world, that darkness flees from the light, and that they who are in God are not afraid of the light. Then, with only the light from my iPhone and another light held by someone else, we began to pray for people and experienced the power of God moving.

You see, the power of God is not limited by music. It's not limited by electricity. It's not limited by any nation or country.

And it certainly wasn't limited by the darkness of Hinduism and Hindu statues all around us.

God is not limited. And He's looking for sons and daughters to flow through. Sons and daughters who will release the power of God. Son and daughters who will go and proclaim the good news of the gospel that the kingdom of God is at hand. Get ready. Heal the sick, raise the dead, cast out demons!

We prayed for a lot of people that night. We found out later that those in attendance couldn't believe we continued preaching after the electricity had gone out. In the past, a minister would quit preaching if the power went off. Well, you can't quit preaching just because the lights go out; you have to adapt to the situation and keep going.

Before leaving Pastor Easu, we told him that we would be back to visit him the following year. We then departed with Jashuva — Evangelist Jashuva — and Pastor Daniel to spend more time with them.

James and I preached in two crusades, to about four to five hundred people a night, as well as in churches and at a two-day pastors' conference. We preached the Kingdom of God, then went out and laid hands on everyone, praying for needs and releasing impartation for them to go and Do The Stuff. We saw the power of God hit them, causing many to fall out under the power and many to receive healing. Those with poor eyesight noticed their vision improving. Those who were hard of hearing began to experience improvement in their hearing. Aches and pains in legs, knees, backs, and hips began to disappear. You could tell by the way their eyes lit up that something powerful was happening.

I'm here to tell you that this gospel is powerful and it's good for the whole world!

One night, we ministered in a Hindu village that had never experienced an open-air gospel meeting before. I preached to about two hundred people that night. People may have come for the singing or the lights, but by simply showing up they received the added benefit of hearing the gospel of Jesus Christ. That night, one hundred forty people stood to receive Jesus as Lord and Savior. James and I then went out and laid hands on all of them.

In the crowd was a teenage girl who told me she had walked six kilometers to get to the meeting because she had heard that people were going to be praying for the sick. In praying for her, I saw God touch her in a powerful way. She then returned home, not by way of some nicely lit street or well-lit sidewalk, but on dirt paths without any lighting.

There are people desperate to hear the gospel and they will travel by whatever means necessary to receive a touch from God; a healing touch. That's what this apostolic call is about: to go to the unreached parts of the earth and release the Kingdom of God. There are people perishing all over this world ... perishing in darkness. There are over a billion people in India, and yet only a small percentage have ever heard the gospel of Jesus Christ.

During the pastors' conference, Pastor Daniel approached me and said he wanted to come under the ministry of GARN. Having experienced the power of God during our time in India, he said that he and other pastors wanted to come under GARN. I said, "Well, that's not why I came here, but that's okay. We can work together." I then said, "At the second day of our ministers conference, we'll ask those pastors there if they want to be a part of GARN India. We will give them the opportunity to join." He said, "That would be good."

There were about sixty ministers at the conference. James and I preached, and the power of God fell. Some of the ministers were baptized in the Holy Spirit. Some received the fire of God.

We had brought with us a number of "fire cloths;" bandanas with a flame print that we had prayed over and were giving out wherever we preached. We had to tear some of them into smaller cloths so there would be enough for people to take home and lay on their sick. Acts 19:11-12 says, "God was performing extraordinary miracles by the hands of Paul, so that handkerchiefs or aprons were even carried from his body to the sick, and the diseases left them and the evil spirits went out." I would later receive testimony of a woman who had a terrible stomach ache late one night. She remembered the fire cloth, laid it on her stomach, and the pain went away.

James and I preached entirely outdoors, in 105- to 110-degree heat with high humidity. My body should have been wasted away. I was tired and sweating. I would get up to preach but felt like I didn't even know what to say. I was worn out. Yet, as I proclaimed the word of God, a transformation would occur ... like Superman in a phone booth. I would become infused with power from on high—"you will receive power when the Holy Spirit has come upon you." The Lord empowered me to preach the gospel.

On the second day of the pastors' conference, toward the end of the day's meeting, I asked those in attendance, "How many want to join with us in GARN ministry with Pastor Daniel who is going to now be Bishop Daniel? He'll be our bishop over India." Fifty-five ministers came forward to say they wanted to be a part of the ministry. James and I laid on hands on them and prayed for them to receive an impartation of the anointing of God that they could take back to their villages and their churches. We anointed Pastor Daniel as Bishop and they recognized me as Apostle over GARN India.

The Indian ministers then set about the task of registering the ministry with the Government of India. Sometime after the conference, more ministers joined, resulting in a total of sixty-three ministers and thirteen churches in India under GARN.

When I decided to make the trip to India, I had no idea it would be the next level, the next step in this apostolic ministry, having just recently resigned from the Assemblies of God and starting GARN. With churches and people of another nation being added to the network, they were coming under GARN's covering and God was confirming my calling.

I believe some who read this book will have an apostolic calling on their lives. God wants to confirm that calling. In fact, He wants to do a work in believers all across America.

Since the first edition of this book, I have returned to India twice, taking with me others who were new to the mission field, some of them having since ventured to Uganda, Africa, to do a work there. On each of the second and third trips to India, we saw a greater number of miracles, signs and wonders than the previous trip. God's power manifested powerfully in Uganda as well. Among other things, GARN has helped provide support and supplies for an orphanage in India; ministerial supplies and transportation for ministers in India; and food for hungry children in India and Africa. We anticipate doing more, even in different parts of the globe, as the Lord directs us and enables us.

At one point during my first visit to India, a group of five young men approached me. One of them said, "Pastor Bill. Ten of us can do what one hundred pastors can do. Send us out. We must go preach the gospel in Afghanistan and Pakistan and Africa!" I'm thinking to myself, *You don't even have shoes on your feet. But you have such a burning desire to preach the gospel.* I believe such passion is passed down to others.

Right now, there is a generation waiting to catch that passion and run with it; a generation of young people looking for spiritual fathers. They are looking for someone who will minister to them, cover them, love them, encourage them, and equip them to preach the gospel. I believe that's what this apostolic calling is about. It's more than just a title. It's about being spiritual fathers and mothers to young men and women that God is calling and raising up. The next generation is looking for someone who will lead the way and not be ashamed of the gospel, for it is the power of God unto the salvation of men. They're looking for leaders who, in addition to not being ashamed, will not become jealous should God raise them up to do even greater exploits than their elders.

Oh, that we could put that generation on our shoulders and lift them up to a level we haven't reached. For the apostolic is not about having everything while preventing others from attaining; it's about our ceiling becoming their floor and lifting them to the next level. We give them an inheritance so they don't have to start at ground zero and we can say to them, "Go and do greater things than we have done." Jesus said to his disciples, "...he who believes in Me, the works that I do, he will do also; and greater works than these he will do; because I go to the Father" (John 14:12).

It's what God is doing in these last days. God is raising up legitimate apostles and prophets, and not necessarily with huge worldwide television and radio ministries either. There are pastors overseeing churches of thousands, and there are pastors just as diligent and faithful, shepherding churches of not more than say, twenty-five apiece.

Why should we think that to be an apostle you must have a world-wide ministry. You might be called to be an apostle over just an area, a community, a county, or at most, a region. There may be apostles tending to many churches, even thousands of churches, while there may be apostles working only two or three churches, if even just one. We should never look at numbers and declare, "Oh, that man's an apostle because he has many churches."

What is God's call on your life? When you look at different ministries, is there one that you are comfortable with? What fits you? Does pastoring fit you? If so, wear it. There's no higher honor or greater badge in being an apostle or a prophet. If you're a prophet, then take that position, put it on, and wear it. Do what God's called you to do. If you're an apostle, don't be ashamed to think of yourself as one.

I believe that an apostle has the ability to function in various ministries, to help with churches, to encourage pastors and other ministers. As an apostle, there may be times when you will have to fill in on a prophetic office or a pastoral office. You may have to operate apostolically over various pastoral places, churches, and ministries.

I believe when you hear that calling from God, the Spirit will grab hold of you and say, "This is what I've called you to do." The Bible says that after an entire night of prayer, Jesus called His disciples and from them chose twelve whom He also named as apostles (see Luke 6:12–13). The apostles were not called by men. They weren't appointed by men. And they certainly weren't voted in by a church board. Jesus called them.

He has called some to be apostles, some to be prophets, some to be evangelists, some to be pastors, and some to be teachers. God will make it clear whether you're called to the work of ministry. God will point out which office or calling you are to fulfill. You may find yourself flowing in more than one. Whatever the case, just walk in the calling of God and don't worry about what people may have to say. You don't have to broadcast who you are. God will identify who you are and confirm what He has spoken to your heart.

What joy resulted in James and I taking the risk to go to India. To risk walking into the unknown. To fly there and be welcomed into a new family — the family of God in India.

Remember the baby I mentioned who had been born shortly before James and I arrived? Before leaving our Indian brothers and sisters to begin our journey home, they said to me, "Pastor, come here. We want to ask you a favor." I said, "What is that?" They said, "Would you give our baby your name?" I said, "What are you talking about?" They said, "Give our baby your name." We held a little celebration service and prayed over the baby. I said, "I give this baby my name: Bill." They said, "Billy Jr." I said, "No, that's really my name, Billy Jr. It would have to be Billy the Third." They said, "No, Junior Billy." So I said, "Okay, Junior Billy."

I now had a spiritual grandson, adopted into the family of God, adopted into my family. Junior Billy of India. And I'm thinking to myself, *I didn't hear the name Junior Billy with any other little kids. So when he's growing up, they're going to be asking, "Why are you named Junior Billy?" He might say, "Oh, because this guy came from America and preached the gospel."*

I pray that I may be such an influence to cause others to say, "I want to be like him. I want to follow in his footsteps." We ought to live life in such a way that others would say, "I want to walk in their footsteps. I want to go and do what they're doing."

There's a battle along the way — trials, tribulations, persecutions, sufferings. There are things that will happen in an attempt to try and stop you in your tracks. We all need encouragement to keep going and not let the trials of life slow us down, for the Lord wants to see what He can trust us with.

Those people in India are precious jewels. The people in Alaska living in remote villages are precious jewels. The Native American people are precious jewels. God needed to see if He could trust me with these people. As I have been faithful in going through trials day to day, God has been faithful to me.

One should not expect God's blessings to be new cars, new houses, or new things, but exceedingly abundant blessings such as being able to visit other countries, preach the gospel, and see signs, wonders and miracles following.

What a blessing it is to be able go to places where people may have never heard the gospel. As we're faithful and obedient to Him, God will say, "I can trust that one. And I can trust that one. I will give them exceedingly and abundantly above and beyond anything they could believe or ask for."

Can He trust that our heads won't get big? Can He trust that we'll stay humble? Can He trust that we will not take advantage of foreigners who would treat us like gods because we've come to them with such great influence and wealth in contrast to what little they have? Can God trust us with those things? Can He trust us to say, "I'm no greater than you, no better than you. I'm just a man like you. Let's sit down together and eat our meals. Let's treat one another with love, respect, and honor as I encourage you to preach and win your people to Jesus."

What a wonderful thing God is doing in these last days by raising up the five-fold ministry. What a blessing to know that at fifty-two years of age my journey was just beginning. A young man from Arkansas named Ross once prophesied over me saying, "God says you've got thirty more years to carry the fire of God." I'm thinking, *Yes! I receive that Lord. Help me.* The ministry is just getting started; it's just beginning to flow in what God has called me to do.

With this calling on my life, I haven't felt comfortable to lay a foundation in any one place and stay put. So far, it's been a mobile ministry. I believe the apostolic is mobile—here a while, there a while, over here, over there—awakening, encouraging, empowering, imparting, and stirring things up.

Various people in the five-fold ministry may experience different callings. My way is not the only way, that's for sure. This is my story of what God has done in my life. I know God has more in store for me and my family in the future as we continue to take the message of AWAKENING, EQUIPPING and IMPARTING—to preach the Kingdom of God.

It's an incredible honor and blessing to be a part of the gospel of Jesus Christ ... to participate in ushering in the Kingdom of God ... to go Do The Stuff ... in Jesus' name. Amen.

Afterword

God bless everybody. I pray this book has edified you, encouraged you, and lifted you up. As of this writing, we reside in Savannah, Tennessee. We've got our homestead here; yet, we're constantly on the road. It's been a privilege to travel across the globe.

It's been a privilege to have young men out of Bible school travel with me. Men like my son-in-law Jonathan Landis, James Richards, Rick Keck, Nick O'Shields, and Daniel Smith. Spiritual sons.

It's been a blessing being connected with revival leaders like Gary and Carol Armstrong, Dan and Carol Vaisanen, Dave and Darla Martini, and Mike and Stephanie Halley. Connections and relationships are important when you are pursuing after revival.

How about getting involved with us to go Do The Stuff, in Jesus' name. "And as you go, preach, saying, 'The kingdom of heaven is at hand.' Heal the sick, raise the dead, cleanse the lepers, cast out demons. Freely you received, freely give" (Matthew 10:7–8).

Bill Easter
Global Apostolic Revival Network
bill@garn.tv
www.garn.tv

Made in the USA
Columbia, SC
05 June 2024

36342086R00096